Innovation und Entrepreneurship

Herausgegeben von
Nikolaus Franke, Wien,
Dietmar Harhoff, München,
Joachim Henkel, München

Innovative Konzepte und unternehmerische Leistungen sind für Wohlstand und Fortschritt von entscheidender Bedeutung. Diese Schriftenreihe vereint wissenschaftliche Arbeiten zu diesem Themenbereich. Sie beschreiben substanzielle Erkenntnisse auf hohem methodischen Niveau.

Herausgegeben von
Professor Dr. Nikolaus Franke,   Professor Dr. Joachim Henkel,
Wirtschaftsuniversität Wien,   Technische Universität München

Professor Dietmar Harhoff, Ph.D.,
Ludwig-Maximilians-Universität München,

Philip Mayrhofer

Interdependencies in the Discovery and Adoption of Facebook Applications

An Empirical Investigation

 Springer Gabler

RESEARCH

Philip Mayrhofer
München, Germany

Dissertation Ludwig-Maximilians-Universität München, 2011

D19

ISBN 978-3-8349-3886-2   ISBN 978-3-8349-3887-9 (eBook)
DOI 10.1007/978-3-8349-3887-9

The Deutsche Nationalbibliothek lists this publication in the Deutsche Nationalbibliografie;
detailed bibliographic data are available in the Internet at http://dnb.d-nb.de.

Library of Congress Control Number: 2012955286

Springer Gabler
© Springer Fachmedien Wiesbaden 2013

Printed on acid-free paper

Springer Gabler is a brand of Springer DE.
Springer DE is part of Springer Science+Business Media.
www.springer-gabler.de

Foreword

Success in the media or entertainment industries is often characterized by a highly skewed distribution: there are few blockbusters and a long tail of unpopular titles. Similar anecdotal evidence has been found for markets for digital products. In his doctoral thesis, Philip Mayrhofer presents one of the first and most comprehensive scientific studies on Facebook Platform, a prominent example of a market for applications.

His work describes in detail the platform's market structure and the distribution of application and developer success rates. The thesis focuses on an empirical analysis of mechanisms which lead to the highly skewed distribution of application usage. In addition to horizontal differentiation and quality differences, he focuses on two forms of interdependencies which may serve as alternative explanations.

First, the author examines whether social processes (interdependencies between users) lead to bandwagon effects. Based on the analysis of individual-level survey data, he finds that social influence, both passive and active, is a strong determinant of a user's decision to adopt an application. Since some applications in addition exhibit increasing returns the more friends are using it, positive and reinforcing processes favor already popular applications.

Second, Philip Mayrhofer examines to which extent lack of information about the choice set of applications contributes to the highly concentrated market structure. In order to study this question, he empirically measures information transfers (interdependencies between applications) that arise when users learn about an application. This may be the case when they discover or use previous applications offered by the developer whose most recent product they have adopted. The results suggest that there are significant, positive spillover effects from the launch of an application on the usage of prior applications. This indicates that consumers would use a larger variety of applications if they knew about them.

Philip Mayrhofer's findings are valuable to a wide range of researchers, especially economists who are interested in the structure of internet-enabled markets. Practitioners will find a thorough description of Facebook Platform and recommendations for the development and marketing of applications.

Munich, October 2012

Prof. Dietmar Harhoff, Ph.D.

Preface

I have many individuals to thank.

Dietmar Harhoff has been a valued advisor and advocate of academic ambition since I first started working with him as student research assistant back in 2003. My foremost gratitude goes to him.

Many people at LMU München have generously offered support throughout this project. Tobias Kretschmer's encouragement in the initial and Georg von Graevenitz' essential guidance and feedback in the final stages are much appreciated. During my stints at INNO-tec, I always felt welcome and supported by my fellow researchers. The conversations with my friend Stefan Wagner made me a better challenger of my own work and Silvia Appelt provided focus and skills when needed. Arnold Picot is an inspirational mentor and Rahild Neuburger an always reliable supporter.

The unfailing enthusiasm of my collaborators Rebecca Ermecke and Jörg Claussen has been critical to the progress of my doctoral thesis. It also would not have been possible without the savvy data extraction work by Matthias Keller und Jakob Keller.

I was fortunate to have been able to spend time at great academic institutions while working on my thesis. Karim Lakhani of Harvard Business School and Eli Noam of Columbia University have been much appreciated hosts and discussion partners. I feel fortunate that my new and renewed friendships with Clemens, Daniel, Geoff, Moritz and Tarek continue to enrich my life. Financial support from the Förderverein Kurt Fordan and the Lothar-and-Sigrid-Rohde-Stiftung is gratefully acknowledged.

Before, during and after my dissertation, working at the Center for Digital Technology and Management (CDTM) has given me tremendous meaning. Uta Weber, Jörg Eberspächer, Yale Braunstein and my fellow CAs have made this time special. Bernhard, Niko and Becci: your cheers at the graduation ceremony will never be forgotten.

I like to thank my friends Albert, Andi, Felix, Gabriel, Jonathan, Lennie, Mulle, Sebi, and Steven - I had your understanding and affirmation when it counted.

This dissertation is wholeheartedly dedicated to my father Johannes, a role-model of intelligence, wit and kindness. He, my mother Waltraud, my sister Anna and my brother Jakob are my fundamental strength. The love and care of Mireia made and makes everything possible.

Philip Mayrhofer

Table of contents

Table of figures

Table of tables

Table of abbreviations

Abbreviations used in the text

API	application programming interface
ATE	average treatment effect
CEO	Chief Operating Officer
CSV	comma-separated values
e.g.	for example
HHI	Herfindahl-Hirsch-Index
HTML	hyper text markup language
i.e.	that is
OLS	ordinary least squares
PHP	hypertext preprocessor
RCM	Rubin causal model
s.d.	standard deviation
SQL	structured query language
WOM	word-of-mouth

Abbreviations used in result tables

'000s	in thousands
'00s	in hundreds
accum.	accumulated
app	application
dev	developer
N	number (of observations), frequency
num.	number
prev.	previous
S.D.	standard deviation

Note: Symbols used in formulas are defined when they occur.

1 Introduction

1.1 Motivation and research objective

Within less than six years of its founding, Facebook has developed from an upstart in online social networking and a phenomenon of growth and user adoption to a platform that has redefined how people worldwide interact with each other. Various research projects have focused on Facebook studying users' identity construction and self presentation (Zhao et al. 2008; Barash et al. 2010; Naaman et al. 2010), reputation in circles of friends (Walther et al. 2008), contagious growth patterns in user membership (Sun et al. 2009), impact of privacy concerns on members' behavior (Acquisti & Gross 2006) and research ethics, sampling and research methodology for social network analysis (Gjoka et al. 2010).

Significantly less research has been dedicated to another platform that Facebook launched several years after its primary, online networking service. In May 2007, Facebook launched a set of programming tools that allowed third-party developers to build and market applications with additional functionality. One year later, developers had launched more than 30,000 applications on the platform and had amassed more than 900 million installations from users. In early 2011, Facebook reports that 2.5 million developers and partners from more than 190 countries have used Facebook Platform and that Facebook users install 20 million applications every day.[1] Research on the Facebook Platform is scarce until now; first studies analyze general characteristics of applications (Gjoka et al. 2008) or social influence in the adoption of applications (Onnela & Reed-Tsochas 2010).

This dissertation studies the Facebook Platform, its developers and application users as well as Facebook's management of the platform in more detail. The many thousand Facebook applications constitute an overwhelmingly large and constantly growing choice set. Early studies and anecdotal evidence suggests that the distribution of success among the many applications is highly skewed - few large applications combine most of the usage.[2] This distribution is common in the media or entertainment industries which are often characterized by few blockbusters and a long-tail (Anderson 2006; Fleder & Hosanagar 2009).

---

[1] Source: Facebook web page on statistics (Facebook 2011b).
[2] See Gjoka et al. (2008) and the analysis of section 3.3.

Economists are interested in highly concentrated markets because they oftentimes bring economic welfare loss (Hendricks & Sorensen 2009). The lack of information about obscure applications represents a welfare loss for individuals who would prefer to use less popular applications if they knew about them. It may also disincentivize developers to build applications that appeal only to few users because they will be difficult to find. This could lead to a focus on mass-compatible applications and, thus, a decrease in product variety.

A skewed distribution of success and high market concentration is commonly explained by horizontal differentiation and quality differences between applications. But other explanations exist as well. One explanation is that social processes and interactions between users are at work that lead to bandwagon effects (Bikhchandani & Hirschleifer 1992; Kretschmer et al. 1999). The other potential explanation is that the lack of information about the choice set, i.e. if consumers are unaware or poorly informed about most products, contributes to the skewness. If either is the case, market demand depends not only on user preferences but also on their knowledge of the product space and the process by which they obtain this knowledge (Hendricks & Sorensen 2009).

The dissertation at hand aims at examining these alternative explanations for concentrated market outcomes in more detail and at unraveling how different sources of information shape demand in the market for Facebook applications. It specifically examines whether there exist interdependent elements in the process by which users get to know applications.[3] For this analysis, a distinction is made between interdependencies that may arise between consumers of products as well as interdependencies between the products themselves. In the following I describe these two research objectives in more detail.

The first objective is to study *interdependencies between users:* an analysis of individual-level decisions in the adoption of Facebook applications. Discovery, adoption and usage in an internet-enabled market in general and on Facebook particularly are increasingly embedded in a social context. Consumers are passively influenced through the visibility of usage patterns in their personal network through reviews, ratings or matching mechanisms (Oestreicher-Singer & Sundararajan 2008; Hervas-Drane 2009).

---

[3] Interdependence is defined as two or more people or things that are dependent on each other (Oxford Dictionaries Online 2011).

Additionally, active forms of social influence exist that take the form of recommendations which are directly conveyed via predominantly digital or online word-of-mouth processes (Katz & Lazarsfeld 1955; Trusov et al. 2009). It is widely acknowledged that in such contexts bandwagon processes – interdependent feedback processes where adoption decisions by some increase the incentive or pressure to adopt for others – are common and may lead to winner-takes-all market outcomes (Katz & Shapiro 1985; Katz & Shapiro 1986; Abrahamson & Rosenkopf 1997).

My study on interdependencies between users is based on individual-level data from a web survey and contributes to existing research in two ways. First, unlike previous studies, I analyze the effect of social influence and network externalities on product adoption simultaneously. Existing studies predominantly focus either on the effect of social influence (Van den Bulte & Stremersch 2004; Aral & Walker 2010) or the effect of network externalities on product adoption (Katz & Shapiro 1985; Corrocher & Zirulia 2009). The choice of a more comprehensive framework (i.e. encompassing both social influence as well as network effects) allows drawing a more refined picture of the user-interdependent mechanisms that lead to positive interdependencies in the adoption of products. Second, the study is not confined to the analysis of product adoption. It also examines the circumstances in which actors who already adopted a new product choose to promote an application by actively exerting influence to stimulate adoption amongst their peers (Subramani & Rajagopalan (2003) and Henkel & Block (2008)). By considering this second decision, the loop of interdependence in the usage of applications is fully closed and the findings may indicate to which extent bandwagon processes work on different levels and become a reinforcing process.

The second objective is to focus on *interdependencies between applications* in form of information transfers that arise between products: consumers discover and learn about a product because of their discovery or consumption of another product created by the same producer. These information spillovers can be distinguished with regard to the direction in which spillovers occur. Backward spillovers describe the process that consumers learn about previous products and forward spillovers refer to consumers who have a product and learn about entirely new products sold by the same producer. The first study on information spillovers between products is the work by Hendricks & Sorensen (2009). The authors analyze album releases in the recorded music industry and quantify to which extent albums lost sales because consumers may not have known them. For their sample they find a positive and persistent effect on the sales of previous catalog albums in the weeks following the release of a new album. The patterns of these sales effects suggest that spillovers result from changes in the consumer's information about available albums and not a change in their preferences or social effects.

To the best of my knowledge, this dissertation is the first empirical analysis of information spillovers between digital products. There are important differences between digital products like Facebook applications and physical products such as compact discs of popular music albums that are sold in brick and mortar stores. Besides differences in search costs and social effects in the discovery and consumption of Facebook applications, the analysis needs to consider that the relevant success metric is not unit sales (or revenues) but usage and time spent with the product. These market conditions are novel and neither empirical evidence nor theoretical models exist for information spillovers in digital markets. Consequently, it is a contribution of this dissertation to adapt the empirical approach to measuring the spillovers by Hendricks & Sorensen (2009) to the context of Facebook applications and to examine whether and to which extent information spillovers occur.

The next section describes how I proceed to answer the research questions of this dissertation.

1.2 Approach

I proceed as follows. This **introduction** continues with section 1.3 that defines important terms and provides the theoretical foundation of the following analyses. The following section 1.4 concludes the introduction by describing the research context in more detail. It introduces general developments on the internet and specifically Facebook as an online social network and platform for applications.

The following **chapter 2** is an in-depth description of the original and unique data set. I describe in detail how the data was captured from the official directory of Facebook applications and how it was processed in order to be suitable for statistical analysis. To the best of my knowledge, the data set is unique with respect to its representativeness of the full population of Facebook applications in the early phase of Facebook Platform. It also contains information and measures not found in comparable data sets.[4] This data set is not only used for the analysis of interdependencies between applica-

---

[4] Compare the empirical studies of Facebook applications by Gjoka et al. (2008) and Onnela & Reed-Tsochas (2010).

tions in the discovery and usage of Facebook applications but is also the basis for several preliminary analyses of secondary interdependencies that provide additional insights into the economic activity on Facebook's platform for applications.

The two main research questions relate to user-centric forms of interdependencies that may have an influence on market concentration and the structure of Facebook's platform for applications. However, there exist other forms of interdependencies on the platform that take a secondary role but are nonetheless important to consider in order to understand the specific market environment on Facebook's platform. In **chapter 3**, I analyze and describe these secondary conditions and interdependencies in detail. I first describe how I sample data from the base data set described in chapter 2. A reduction from the population of applications is necessary in order to ensure that consistent data is available for all analyses and that outliers which may distort the analyses are excluded from the data. In the following I analyze the impact that actions by Facebook as the operator of the platform have on the way applications are adopted and used. It is important to examine this case because it shows how the interdependencies between users (which are analyzed in chapter 4), are influenced by the decisions of a third party, here Facebook as platform operator. In this chapter I also study the management of Facebook applications and specifically the interdependence within a developer's portfolio: the time that elapses between application launches. This question is of relevance because it provides insights into the decision making of developers and whether the launch of a new application is influenced by the previous application's success or growth path as well as other developer or market characteristics. The findings from these analyses and descriptions serve as valuable background for the following specific analyses of interdependencies in the discovery and adoption of Facebook applications.

Chapter 4 presents the individual-level study on interdependencies between users. Based on data from an online survey, it examines to which extent social influence and the perception of network effects impact individual decisions in the context of Facebook applications. The two decisions under investigation are (1) the decision to adopt and use an application and (2) the decision of whether to promote and exert influence on friends to also use the application. The findings from this analysis contribute to answering the question of whether interdependencies between users, such as bandwagon processes, are responsible for concentrated market outcomes.

The interdependence between applications in the usage of Facebook applications is studied in **chapter 5**. This analysis examines to which extent spillovers between applications within the portfolio of one developer exist. Here, different mechanisms in which information spillovers may occur are conceptually discussed and a method is described which allows measuring the spillovers based on a clearly identifiable event. The results of this analysis help to assess the effect of information about available options in the market for Facebook applications on the structure of the market.

In the final **chapter 6**, I summarize the findings of the previous studies and discuss their contribution to the debate on market structure in internet-enabled industries.

1.3 Definitions and theoretical foundation

This section provides the theoretical foundation for the following chapters. It starts out with a definition and classification of interdependencies in the discovery and adoption of products on the internet (section 1.3.1). It then describes each of the two forms of interdependence in more detail by focusing first on users (section 1.3.2) and later on applications (section 1.3.3).

1.3.1 Discovery and adoption of products on the internet

The objective of this dissertation is an empirical analysis of the discovery and adoption of Facebook applications. Applications can be seen as cultural online goods which provide recreational value (Onnela & Reed-Tsochas 2010). Two typical characteristics of cultural industries include oversupply of consumption goods and ex-ante uncertainty about product quality (Kretschmer et al. 1999). In such markets, consumers are often poorly informed about the majority of the available products – especially new products. As a result, demand depends not only on consumer preferences and product quality, but also on the knowledge about the available options. Knowledge about a product is, therefore, critical in the consumer decision-making process: in the first place, it is important that consumers learn about the existence of a product and become aware of it ("the discovery"). Secondly, it matters what exactly and from whom consumers learn about the product in order to make their purchase decision (Hendricks & Sorensen 2009; Hendricks et al. 2009).

The following chapters contain analyses that focus on the process in which consumers get to know Facebook applications. They specifically examine whether there exist interdependent elements in this process.[5] Here, a distinction is made between interdependencies that may arise between consumers of products as well as interdependencies between the products themselves. The following sections define both forms of interdependence in more detail.

1.3.2 Interdependencies between users

The following sections provide the terminology which serves as a basis for the remaining chapters. Interdependencies between users can be classified along two different categories. On the one hand, consumers influence each other in their purchasing decisions regardless of the type of product that they are consuming. This makes each individual's behavior a function of the behavior of other consumers (see section 1.3.2.1). On the other hand, interdependencies in the purchasing decision also depend on particular product characteristics that link the utility of a user to the number of other consumers of the goods, i.e. so-called network externalities (see section 1.3.2.2).

Due to the empirical context of the dissertation, hereafter consumers will be referred to as users and products as applications. The effect of both forms of interdependence on the adoption of Facebook applications is studied in chapter 4.

1.3.2.1 Social influence

Research on social influence originates from research in social psychology which focuses particularly on micro-level processes among individuals.[6] I define social influence broadly as the ways in which people affect each others' beliefs, feelings, and behaviors (Mason et al. 2007). It is broadly established that consumer choice is influenced in a direct and meaningful way by the actions taken by others. Such influence can stem from e.g. the "action" of face-to-face recommendation to a friend but can also result from the observation of what a stranger is doing (Godes et al. 2005).[7] Consequently, I distinguish between two types of social influence. I refer to the former as

---

[5] Interdependence is defined as two or more people or things that are dependent on each other (Oxford Dictionaries Online 2011).

[6] However, researchers from other fields, like economics, have also begun to develop theoretical models. See Mason et al. (2007) for a review of models of social influence from a number of fields. The authors discuss different dimensions on which the models differ and recommend specific types that they regard to be most promising for further research.

[7] Godes et al. (2005) refer to such activities as "social interactions". Another common term is "social learning" which refers to any mechanism through which individuals learn from each other (Cai et al. 2009).

active social influence because the originator or source of influence is actively and intentionally influencing another individual. The latter is referred to as *passive social influence* because the originator is not necessarily aware that his actions are influencing other individuals.

A prominent example for this distinction is provided by Becker (1991). When choosing between two restaurants, an individual may be heavily influenced by the opinions and experiences of his friends or by simply observing how many customers are already in each restaurant - even without knowing their identities and reasons for choosing the restaurant. The theory for the former type of opinion- or preference-based social interaction is commonly defined as *word-of-mouth* (WOM). The boundaries around the definition of WOM are, however, illdefined (Godes et al. 2005). A first conceptualization of the phenomenon and the most narrow definition was introduced by Katz & Lazarsfeld (1955) and Granovetter (1973). Here, WOM entailes the one-to-one and face-to-face exchange of information about a product or service. WOM, is a more established construct in the marketing literature (Arndt 1967), where it, more generally, refers to the dissemination of information (e.g., opinions and recommendations) via communication among individuals. Recent technological developments (like email and mobile communications) led to a broadening of the traditional definition. It now includes communication and interaction that is direct but not necessarily simultaneous or face-to-face (Godes et al. 2005).

The latter type of action- or behavior-based social interaction in the restaurant example is commonly referred to as *observational learning* and its study originated in the psychology as well as the information cascade theory in the economics literature (Bikhchandani et al. 1998). According to this theory, information from observational learning contains signals expressed by the actions of other consumers, but not the reasons behind their actions. Under the assumption of limited information, publicly available information that consumers gather from the history of all previous purchase actions from other individuals outweighs their own private information in shaping their beliefs. Eventually, an information cascade may arise because subsequent observers will hold similar beliefs. As a result, people may engage in a type of "herd behavior" (Banerjee 1992) by following their predecessors' actions.

Recent developments in technology, like consumer reviews and matching mechanisms on e-commerce web sites, have created communication forms that blur the boundaries between WOM and observational learning. Here, information exchanged between consumers shares many common features with traditional WOM, even though it is both anonymous and one-to-many in nature (Godes & Mayzlin 2004; Dellarocas 2003; Chen & Xie 2008).[8] In general, one must be cautious about using findings on social influence on the internet to derive implications for broader social interactions (Godes et al. 2005). For example, it is not established to which extent online activities of social influence are a proxy for their offline analogs.[9] In the context of this dissertation, however, both the social interaction and the following adoption decision are made in an online environment. As a consequence, the problem of transferring influence from one context to the other does not apply.

1.3.2.2 Network externalities

It is important to distinguish social influence from network externalities, another mechanism that also results in conformative or herd behavior.[10] Social influence, in the definition of this dissertation, assumes that individuals care about other peoples' actions only because the actions convey information about the quality of a product. By contrast, network externalities imply that each consumer's utility from a good depends directly on the consumption of the good by others. Such a utility gain can be explained with the "technical" characteristics of a product that make it more useful when consumed jointly. Direct network effects result from interaction possibilities with other consumers of the product. They typically relate to technical interaction possibilities such as the ability to do calls with a mobile phone. In the context of cultural goods like applications or music, however, externalities can also arise because people like dis-

---

[8] More recent research examines the consequences on market concentration and structure in theoretical (Hervas-Drane 2009) and in empirical studies (Dellarocas & Narayan 2007; Oestreicher-Singer & Sundararajan 2008; Oestreicher-Singer & Sundararajan 2009).

[9] However, online social networks offer a rich set of data for empirical researchers (see for example the study by Onnela & Reed-Tsochas (2010) based on aggregate Facebook data). The fundamental differences between online and offline social interactions (e.g., anonymity and speed of diffusion) provide an interesting research area.

[10] Network externalities are in the following interchangeably referred to as network effects. See Rohlfs (1974) for one of the first definitions of network externalities. The author noticed that in communication services, the utility a subscriber derives from a product increases as others join the network. This can be categorized as external economies of consumption (externalities) because a new adopter does not internalize the positive effect on others in her adoption decision. Katz & Shapiro (1985) generalize the idea adding examples from other industries. The authors further distinguish between direct and indirect network externalities. Indirect network externalities refer to the availability of compatible products (see section 1.3.3).

cussing movies with friends. The utility from watching a movie that others in the peer group have seen is higher than the utility of watching the same movie when no one else in the peer group has seen it (Kretschmer et al. 1999; Moretti 2009). Furthermore, global and local network effects can be distinguished (Koski & Kretschmer 2004; Corrocher & Zirulia 2009). Global network externalities are in place when an individual only cares about the total number of other consumers. Local network externalities occur when an individual is only interested in a particular subset of other consumers, e.g. his or her friends. In the context of Facebook applications, a network externality arises when a consumer's utility of using an application depends directly on the number of friends who also use the application. Thus, the network externalities of interest are typically direct and local.

1.3.3 Interdependencies between applications

The dissertation also focuses on the examination of processes in which the information about the existence of a product depends on the knowledge about the existence of a related product. In the specific case of Facebook, I am interested in interdependencies between the applications of one particular developer. This type of interdependence is here defined as information spillover between products and is reviewed in the following section 1.3.3.1. In order to make the definitive distinction from other forms of interdependencies between products, related literature, namely the literature on brand spillovers and complementarities, is discussed in section 1.3.3.2.

1.3.3.1 Information spillovers

In the context of this dissertation interdependence between applications is focused on information spillovers between products: consumers discover and learn about a product because of their discovery or consumption of another product sold by the same producer. These information spillovers can be distinguished with regard to the direction in which spillovers occur. Backward spillovers describe the process that consumers learn about products previously released to the one that they are initially using; forward spillovers refer to consumers who have a product and learn about newly released products from the same producer.

The main and to the best of the author's knowledge only study on information spillovers between products is the work by Hendricks & Sorensen (2009). The authors analyze album releases in the recorded music industry and quantify to which extent albums lost sales because consumers may not have known them. For their sample they find a positive and persistent effect on the sales of previous catalog albums in the weeks following the release of a new album. The patterns of these sales effects suggest that spillovers result from changes in the consumer's information about available albums and not a change in their preferences or social effects. The study uses data from a time when the discovery of new albums was primarily mediated by radio and consumers purchased hard disk albums at brick-and-mortar stores. The scarcity of air-time on the radio created an informational bottleneck in which consumers listened typically to the most popular albums, which is only a small fraction of all available albums.

The study by Hendricks & Sorensen (2009) on spillovers between music albums is based on data prior to the dominance of digital music and the distribution of albums via the internet. In the discussion of their findings, the authors argue that the internet may change the occurrence and magnitude of information spillovers. On the internet consumers gather information about products more easily and have the opportunity to sample the music before a purchase. Today, the radio as broadcast medium or the display of albums in brick and mortar stores do not play an equally important role for the discovery of new music. The authors expect that, as a result of this easier access to information, spillovers become smaller. This again leads to increased variety of albums in the market and also a less skewed distribution of success.[11] Details on the empirical approach by Hendricks & Sorensen (2009) as well as a discussion of information spillovers in the context of Facebook applications are provided in chapter 5.

1.3.3.2 Brand spillovers and complementarities

Information spillovers are a novel strand of research in the economics and management literature. The two traditional aspects of interdependencies between products covered in the literature are brand spillovers as well as "technical" complementarities between products which affect the demand for each product.[12] I discuss these strands of literature briefly in order to distinguish them from the definition of information spillovers as form of interdependence between products.

---

[11] In a recent working paper, Hendricks & Sorensen (2009) develop theoretical models of market demand in which consumers learn about products by observing the decisions of other consumers, which is the case in internet markets and online social platforms such as Facebook.

[12] These two types of interdependencies are not in the focus of this dissertation but are discussed as alternative explanations for the findings in chapter 5, which analyzes information spillovers between applications.

The closest to information spillovers in the spirit of Hendricks & Sorensen (2009) is the economics literature on brand spillovers. Wernerfelt (1988), Choi (1998) and Cabral (2000) have developed theoretical models that study the impact of spillovers on firms' decisions with regard to whether to release new products under existing brand names. When consumers are uncertain about product qualities, the strong reputation of an existing product increases demand for new products sold under the same brand (forward spillover), and the release of a high-quality new product can improve the brand image and boost sales of the existing product (backward spillover).

Markets which are characterized by systems of components are examined in the "systems market" literature, a stream within the field of industrial organization of economic research (Farrell & Saloner 1986; Katz & Shapiro 1985; Ellison & Ellison 2005; Tucker & Zhang 2010). Common examples for system markets are DVD players and DVDs, video game consoles and games, the personal computing ecosystem, and camera and film. Research in the field is concerned with market dynamics when the demand for one product is dependent upon factors other than its intrinsic price or technical characteristics. Here, interdependencies in demand can arise because of complementary characteristics that increase the utility of each product. In this case, one speaks of indirect network externalities.

After this brief introduction to definitions and theoretical concepts, I now turn to a description of the research context.

1.4   Research context

This section introduces the research context of the dissertation.[13] It describes recent developments on the internet in section 1.4.1 and provides a detailed introduction to Facebook and its platforms in section 1.4.2.

Facebook is the world's largest online social networking service with over 550 million active users as of January 2011.[14] The website is operated by privately held Facebook Incorporated, a company headquartered in Palo Alto, California and lead by co-

---

[13] This section is an extract from an unpublished paper by Mayrhofer & Keller (2011) that describes the background and process of data collection from Facebook's directory of applications in detail (see also chapter 2).

[14] The empirical analysis of Facebook applications and developers (see chapter 0 and chapter 5) uses data of the period from September 2007 to June 2008. The survey of users for the analysis of chapter 4 was conducted in February 2008. At that time, Facebook had between 40 and 70 million active users (see Figure 2).

founder and CEO Mark Zuckerberg.[15] Currently, in mid 2011, the online social network Facebook is at its height in terms of popular and media attention. Mark Zuckerberg was named Person of the Year 2010 by Time Magazine (Grossman 2010) for "connecting more than half a billion people and mapping the social relations among them, for creating a new system of exchanging information and for changing how we live our lives". Earlier this year, Facebook dominated the news when it raised additional funds of 500 million US dollars in a private round led by Goldman Sachs and at a valuation of 50 billion US dollars (Craig & Sorkin 2011; Ahmed 2011).[16]

1.4.1 Background

There are two recent developments on the internet that are of particular importance for the context of this dissertation: the emergence of (1) online social networks and of (2) platforms for third-party programs. Based on these developments, markets with an overwhelming supply of applications were established in very short time and the consumption of these applications is taking place in increasingly socially embedded contexts. Facebook is driving both developments actively and it is important to understand the context for an interpretation of the results of the following empirical studies.

Emergence of online social networks

Over the last few years, software tools that facilitate social interaction on the internet have become increasingly common. Prominent examples for this type of web site are Facebook, MySpace and LinkedIn. Such services are generally known as online social networks[17] which "allow individuals to (1) construct a public or semi-public profile within a bounded system, (2) articulate a list of other users with whom they share a connection, and (3) view and traverse their list of connections and those made by others within the system" (Boyd & Ellison 2007).[18]

---

[15] See Crunchbase (2011) for a continuously updated web page with information and news on the company (including the most recent investor list).
[16] Not to neglect is the attention Facebook received due to the motion picture "The Social Network", which tells an unauthorized and arguably fictional account of the founding story of Facebook. It won four Golden Globe awards (Cieply & Barnes 2011).
[17] Online social networks are also known as "social networking sites", "social networks" or other combinations. The terms are generally used interchangeably.
[18] Boyd & Ellison (2007) provide a comprehensive review of the history of different online social network sites.

In light of the rampant growth in usage of online social networks, research has begun to examine various aspects of the phenomenon. One finding is that connections between users are made primarily between people who have previously met offline rather than novel, online-only connections (Lampe et al. 2006). DiMicco & Millen (2007) explore how Facebook members manage their identity as part of different social groups and find that Facebook usage is likely to become an integral part of the workplace – with both positive and negative consequences. Joinson (2008) analyzes the ways members use and benefit from Facebook. Another group of studies analyzes usage patterns of members of online social networking systems as well as privacy implications of online social networks. For example, Acquisti & Gross (2006) find that privacy concerns play a role in the adoption decision of Facebook, but only for the non-college demographic. Dwyer et al. (2007) compare perceptions of trust and privacy concerns of MySpace and Facebook users. They find similar levels of privacy concerns for both sites, but greater trust in Facebook and its members. The study further demonstrates that trust and privacy safeguards are no prerequisite for the development of online relationships.

Emergence of platforms for third-party programs

A second development relates to the emergence of software platforms on the internet as a toolkit for third-party developers and "engine" for industries and eco-systems (Evans et al. 2006). Since the early days of the Web, people have shared and embedded small software programs that add interactivity in their web sites (these programs are often referred to as "widgets"). Today, widgets are frequently found on personal web sites, blogs and increasingly on profile pages of online social networking sites.[19] The ability to personalize a user's profile page by adding widgets played an important role in the success of MySpace (Boyd & Ellison 2007). Slide and RockYou!, now two of the largest developers of Facebook applications, were amongst the first companies to develop widgets specifically for MySpace.[20] Despite the fact that MySpace initially did not officially support these widgets, and at times even tried to sanction them, they

---

[19] Widgets are also often used as form of advertising since they are far more effective in attracting the interest of internet users than classical banner advertisements. For this reason, they are increasingly used as part of online marketing campaigns (Yared 2008). Numerous development companies are specializing on the creation of such widgets.

[20] RockYou! was originally known as RockMySpace, suggesting that it provided tools to personalize and improve users' MySpace profile pages.

became immensely popular with users (Lee 2007). The role of widgets on social net-working sites is limited to enabling users to personalize their profile pages. Widgets do not have access to data about the user's friends nor can they use the communication channels of the social networking site.

The next section describes how this approach was fundamentally challenged when Facebook turned itself into a platform and allowed for social applications to take the place of widgets.

1.4.2 Facebook

This section describes the different platforms that Facebook built and operates and which played in important role in the tremendous success of Facebook.[21]

Facebook as a multi-sided platform

Facebook's original and main service is a consumer-oriented social network that maps out "real and pre-existing connections among people" (The Economist 2007) and facilitates their interaction. Over the years, however, it has evolved into a firm that operates what is often referred to as a multi-sided network or platform (Boudreau & Hagiu 2010).[22] Platforms are products, services or technologies that serve as foundations upon which other parties can build complementary products, services or technologies (Gawer & Cusumano 2002). A multi-sided platform serves more than one group and is both a platform and a market intermediary (Hagiu 2007).[23] In addition to its platform for individual "members", Facebook brings together advertisers, commercial business members, content suppliers, and applications software developers.

---

[21] The most comprehensive account of Facebook's founding story is presented in Kirkpatrick (2010). A detailed description of the Facebook Platform is provided by Eisenmann et al. (2009).

[22] For more literature on two-sided and multi-sided markets, see the following studies in the field of economics and management (Katz & Shapiro 1994; Parker & Van Alstyne 2005; Eisenmann et al. 2006; Rochet & Tirole 2006).

[23] Other examples for multi-sided platforms or networks are: Sony's PlayStation, Visa credit cards, Microsoft's Windows, or eBay.

Figure 1: Schematic illustration of Facebook as a multi-sided platform[24]

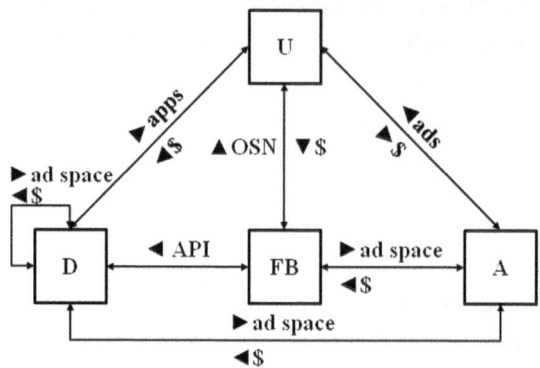

Figure 1 illustrates this platform eco-system. The stylized arrows in the graphic show the direction of an activity. Facebook (FB) is the intermediary that enables interaction between the different groups. It provides users (U) with an online social network (OSN), advertisers (A) with an advertising space on the service, and developers (D) with the technical infrastructure (API: application programming interface) to develop add-on programs. The graphic also shows additional exchange relationships. For example, much of the economic value is generated by revenue that Facebook and application developers make by offering space for advertisers to promote their products and services. While the membership to Facebook is free-of-charge for users, Facebook and application developers receive income from a small portion of users who purchase virtual gifts and goods. The management of the many stakeholders is a sizable challenge. In many cases, incentives of different groups are not aligned and Facebook needs to impose rules and regulations that balance the interests of all parties involved.[25]

The following sections provide more background on Facebook's core service, the platform for social interaction of users (i.e. the online social network) as well as the platform for applications that are developed by third-party developers.

---

[24] Source: own illustration.
[25] A description and analysis of change to the rules of the platform made by Facebook in early 2008 is provided in section 0.

Facebook as an online social network

Facebook was launched as a consumer-oriented social network that facilitates interaction between its users. At first, access was restricted to students at Harvard, but huge demand prompted Facebook to open up to several other U.S. universities within a few months. Over the course of the following years, Facebook kept growing its user base by incrementally granting access to new groups of users: students from colleges across the U.S. and Canada (2004/2005), high-school students (September 2005), students of international schools (October 2005), employees of selected corporations (May 2006), and finally everyone (September 2006). Beginning early 2008, the website was translated into an increasing number of languages other than English, which helped spur international growth (Crunchbase 2011). Figure 2 illustrates the impressive growth in users and gives a timeline of events that are of particular importance in the context of this dissertation.

While the number of registered users was growing, Facebook focused on improving its website. Since the beginning, Facebook was a social networking site, as defined by Boyd & Ellison (2007): the basic functionality of Facebook enables individuals to create a personal profile page that contains information about them, including e-mail address, favorite movies and a profile picture. Users express their relationship with others by becoming "friends" and spend time browsing other users' profile pages. The ability to communicate through private messages is another core feature. Facebook soon started to add a string of further features.

The most relevant for the study here are the News Feed and Mini-Feed (September 2006).[26] The Mini-Feed collects "stories" of each user and lists them on his profile page. Stories are small snapshots of his activities and thoughts via text, sometimes accompanied by photos, web links, or videos. The updates are similar to those seen on micro-blogging services such as Twitter and, in fact, many users re-direct one to the other. Stories are "automated broadcast notifications" (Aral & Walker 2010) because Facebook forwards the stories to the user's social network. The News Feed collects all stories from a user's social network and offers a kind of perpetual contact with one's

---

[26] See Facebook (2011a) for a timeline of events and feature launch dates. Other important features were Mobile (April 2006), Notes (August 2006), Share (November 2006), virtual gift shop (February 2007), network portals (April 2007), Marketplace (May 2007), and Chat (April 2008). Facebook's usage of capitalization for key terms such as "Wall" and "Page" is adopted throughout this text.

social network (Joinson 2008). The concept of stories that are broadcasted and collected is important for the following empirical analyses because these features are the basis for observational learning about other users' activities and, thus, an important channel through which social influence is exerted.[27]

Figure 2: Facebook timeline with important milestones[28]

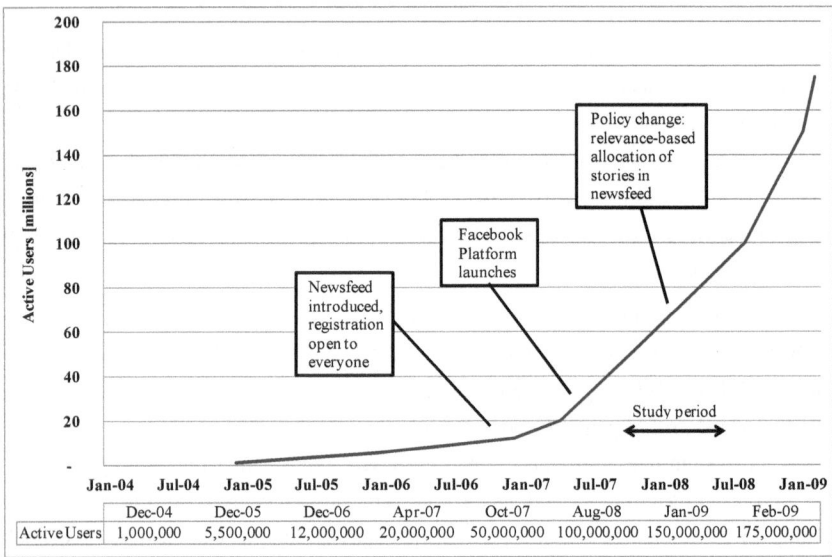

Facebook as a platform for applications

Some of the additional features launched by Facebook were referred to early on as applications, a term that reflects their character as modular complements to Facebook's core functionality. For example, Facebook launched the Photos application in October 2005, making it one of the first applications available on Facebook (Crunchbase 2011). A key differentiator of the Photos application is tagging, a feature that lets users annotate pictures with meta information, namely the identity of persons shown. This infor-

---

[27] There is some recent research on the role of the News Feed in the diffusion of messages (Sun et al. 2009) and information overload due to the mass of stories being produced by large groups of connected friends (Günther et al. 2010).

[28] Source: own illustration based on Keller (2009). Note: the figure is based on information collected from Facebook's press releases on the company timeline (Facebook 2011a).

mation is used extensively by the Photos application, e.g. to notify Facebook users when new pictures of themselves or their friends are uploaded or to compile an album of all pictures of a certain person (regardless of who took or uploaded the picture) for display on that person's profile page.

Applications like Photos are an important driver of user activity. They are highly engaging and help increase the number of visitors as well as the average duration of each visit to the Facebook website (Freiert 2007). Despite (or encouraged by) the success of its own applications, Facebook realized that it could further increase usage and thus potential advertisement revenues by opening up to external application developers. Figure 2 shows that the number of active Facebook users has been growing at a much quicker pace since the launch of Facebook Platform in May 2007. The first step in this direction was done in August 2006, when a limited version of the Facebook development platform was launched. Facebook opened up to third-party developers in a radical way with the launch of the Facebook Platform at the F8 event in May 2007. Since the end of 2008, external websites can use Facebook Connect to add social features and integrate with Facebook. Some industry experts go as far as to describe Facebook Platform as an "operation system for the internet" (Schonfeld 2008).

Facebook Platform may be described as a toolkit that allows users with a minimum set of programming skills to innovate. Facebook takes a number of steps to attract developers and reduce barriers to entry. Besides publishing extensive documentation concerning its APIs, the company also makes available programming libraries that facilitate the implementation of new applications and shares the source code of sample applications with developers. "Facebook Developer Garages" are gatherings of local developers and enable the exchange of ideas and experiences. Furthermore, the company partnered with web hosting provider Joyent to offer one year of free server capacity to developers of Facebook applications (Joyent 2011) and even provides financing to start-up companies that develop for Facebook Platform through its "fbFund" (fbFund 2011).

As of now, little research has been published on complementary applications to social networking platforms. This is hardly surprising, considering that the first social networking platform along with third-party applications was launched fairly recently, in May 2007. To date, only few notable academic papers have been published that focus on Facebook applications. For example, Nazir et al. (2008) conduct an experiment to analyze the structure of user interactions on Facebook applications. Furthermore, academic literature that addresses potential success factors for applications is very sparse at this time. Gjoka et al. (2008) are among the first who aim at characterizing the properties of social networking applications.

2 Capture and curation of a data set on Facebook applications

2.1 Chapter overview

An important and extensive part of this dissertation consisted of building an original data set on Facebook developers and applications. With the start of the platform in May 2007, Facebook introduced a directory in which applications were listed, on a daily basis, with information on their functionality, their developers, their usage, and user reviews. The directory with all applications was openly accessible and was used by Facebook users to browse and discover new applications. However, Facebook did not provide an interface for accessing the information contained in the directory. Early on, developer entry rates to the platform suggested large numbers of applications which meant that data could not be collected manually but that an automated approach had to be chosen.

The opportunity of developing a novel and unique data set on digital products was realized by the author at the time of the launch of the Facebook platform in late May 2007. Since an automated approach had to be developed to collect the data from the directory, I approached Matthias Keller, a trained computer scientist, and we jointly developed a strategy to build the data set. There were several objectives. First, data collection was intended to begin as soon as possible in order to capture the dynamic early stages of the nascent market. Second, data should be collected on a daily basis, the same frequency as Facebook updated the data. Third, new applications and developers had to be discovered constantly in order to achieve a full representation of the market. Fourth, the raw data was to be saved locally in order to document the process and to be able to extract different elements at later stages.

The strategy of building the data set for economic analysis was structured in different stages which were based on approaches commonly employed in data-intensive science (Tansley 2009): the capture, the curation, and the analysis of the data. This chapter describes the first two activities of this process. The step of *data capture* involved automated programs known as "web crawlers" that automatically identified the applications in the directory and stored a web page for each application. Furthermore, an automated "parser" extracted the relevant data from the web pages and stored them in a data base. In the *data curation* step, the raw data was further processed and prepared for the subsequent empirical analysis.

The first step of the development of the web crawler was performed in parallel to the dynamically changing market. The design and implementation of the crawler was complicated by Facebook's frequent changes to the design and structure of the directory. Also, the number of applications, for which Facebook generates separate web pages dynamically, was steadily and rapidly increasing. It took several iterations of development and testing until a stable version of the program was in place: consistent data collection started on July 2, 2007. In the next step, the program that extracts the data from the collected and saved web pages (the "parser") was developed. Due to several changes by Facebook to the design and structure of the directory, this parser was improved in several iterations, the last update being implemented in September 2009. The parser was mainly developed by Jakob Keller and its scripts are in detail documented in Keller (2009). The last step of curating the data was also an iterative process which was performed by the author. In several steps, preliminary analyses of the export data identified inconsistencies in the data. Based on these findings, the parser had to be adapted and run repeatedly on the raw data collected from the crawler.[29] A detailed description of the steps taken in each of the three phases is given later in this chapter.

The resulting data set consists of more than 32,000 applications that were active on the Facebook platform in the period from July 2, 2007 to June 30, 2008. It captures the development of the platform and provides time-series data on the application-level for the interesting period of the first year since the launch of the platform.[30] In the following, I discuss the features and limitations of the data set.

The data set is a unique collection of the population of products in a digital market. Due to the approach of capturing the data, the data set is superior to many data sets that are usually compiled in retrospective. It offers a nearly complete account of all entities: applications which are active and "alive" but also the ones which are diminishing, failing, or exiting. Consequently, the data set at hand does not exhibit survivor bias that is a caveat to many studies that rely on data early in the lifetime of a firm or

---

[29] Due to the large number of web pages retrieved by the crawler of which each had to be parsed individually, one run of the parser in the last iteration in September 2009 took more than five weeks.

[30] The only notable drawback of the data set is that it does not cover the first six weeks of observations between the launch of Facebook Platform and the beginning of data collection.

product.[31] Another notable feature of the data set is the variety of variables that it contains. It covers not only basic information about applications, such as their name, description and category, but also usage metrics, information about their developers, a complete download of application Wall and discussion board entries as well as various other attributes. This feature alone differentiates the data set from the ones used in other studies on Facebook applications. It appears unlikely that a comparable data set exists outside of Facebook itself since other recent studies are based on smaller data sets of Facebook application data. For example, Gjoka et al. (2008) initially attempted to collected data from the Facebook application directory, but ultimately decided to rely on an alternative data source. Onnela & Reed-Tsochas (2010), who study the effect of social influence on the adoption of applications, limit their data set to 2,720 applications and the time period from June 25 to August 14, 2007.[32]

A limitation of the data set is caused by the challenging environment for the capture of the data. The design of the crawler retrieves data for applications only, when they are discovered in the application directory on that same day. Since it is not possible to make up for missed observations at a later time, it is unclear how many applications and observations are missing. However, it is unlikely and exploratory analyses do not suggest that applications are systematically missing. Also the number of applications in the data set compared with reports from Facebook and industry observers indicate that most and particularly the major applications are represented in the data set. As a consequence, one can assume that the data set as captured and later reduced is a meaningful representation of the overall population of Facebook applications.

The remainder of this chapter is structured as follows. In section 2.2, I describe the structure and content of the Facebook application directory and individual application pages in the directory. The process of capturing the data from the source as well as the resulting raw data set is described in section 0. Section 2.4 covers the additional steps of data curation which are necessary to arrive at a data set which can be used for the empirical analyses.

---

[31] Data problems in form of survivor bias are often found in studies of first-mover advantage and are discussed in different review articles (Golder & Tellis 1993; VanderWerf & Mahon 1997).

[32] Others studies on Facebook focus on user networks and interactions, not applications and developers (Acquisti & Gross 2006; Lampe et al. 2007; Stutzman 2010).

2.2   Data source

This section describes the Facebook directory of applications and the application directory page. Both are sources from which the data is captured and extracted.

Figure 3 provides a screenshot of the Facebook application directory ("directory") at the time at which data was collected for this study.[33] It lists applications by different characteristics such as "newest" or "most active users". It also allows users to browse 22 different categories of applications. The directory contains a categorized list of all applications that were approved by Facebook. Submitting an application to the directory is free of charge and requires only a few clicks on behalf of the developer. The review is done by Facebook staff and is based on the function of the application, the inclusion of an appropriate icon as well as a couple of test users. Facebook does not consider quality, (brand) name or the possibility that a similar applications is in the directory already. Also, Facebook does not take any responsibility for the developer's actions on the directory page.

While it is not obligatory for developers to apply to list their application in the directory, there are no reasons for developers to choose to be not listed and I am not aware of any instances in which developers did. In fact, when there were some delays in the approval process during the first weeks of the platform, developers chose to release their application and list them in "underground" directories. These applications were approved later on and eventually appeared in the directory.

In addition to the directory, each Facebook application has a dedicated directory page which contains information about the application and tools for users to rate and discuss the application ("application page"). An exemplary application page is provided in Figure 4.[34]

Each application's directory page consists of different elements that provide the data for this data set. It contains basic information such as application name, developer name and profile/website link, a short description of the application's functionality as well as the categories which this application is assigned to within Facebook (see (1) in

---

[33] The design and presentation of the directory has changed since the time period that this study examines.

[34] Note that the design and content of directory and the application page has changed since the time period that this study examines. The application page of Figure 4 was saved in March 2008 and represents the design and content for the period from May 2007 until June 2008.

Figure 4). This information is edited by the developer of the application. Additional information is available for the usage of the application (see (2)). Facebook displays both the number of active users (per day; i.e. 24h)[35] and the percentage of active users of all of the application's installations. These measures based on user engagement displaced the reporting of number of total installations 14 weeks after the platform's launch. The page also has elements in which users of the application can leave a note on the virtual blackboard ("Wall"), write a review or join the discussion forum (see (3)).

The process of how the data from the directory and the application page was captured and further processed is described in the following section.

Figure 3: Screenshot of the Facebook application directory with 22 categories

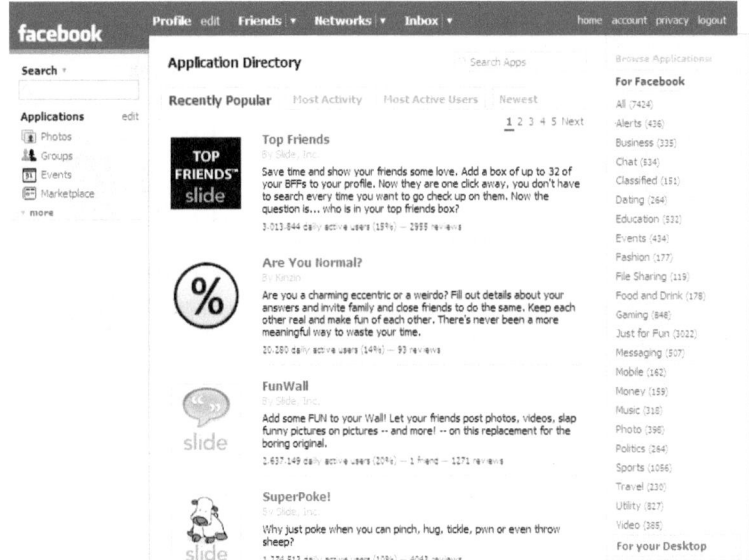

[35] Here active usage is defined by Facebook as a user having actively interacted with the application within the previous day, midnight to midnight. See the announcement on the Facebook developer blog for details (Facebook 2007a).

Figure 4: Screenshot of exemplary application directory page

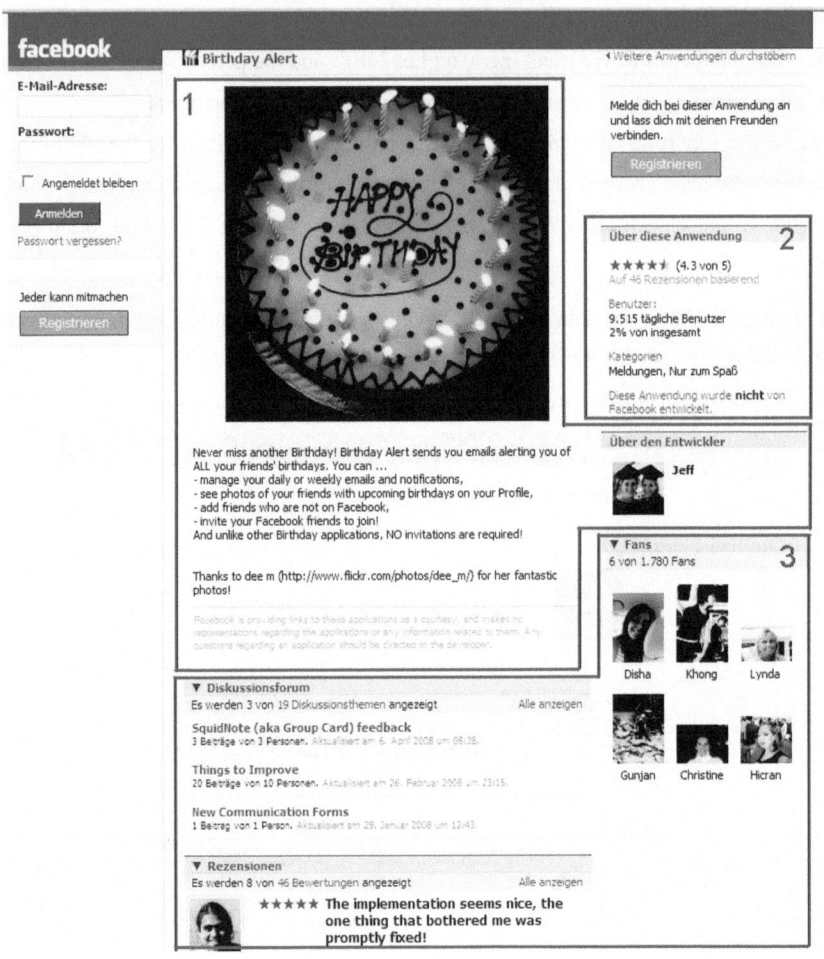

2.3 Data capture

This section describes how the data from the above introduced data source is captured. First, section 2.3.1 provides details on the three distinct steps of the data capture process. Second, section 2.3.2 provides an overview and description of the data files that are the result of the data capture process.

2.3.1 Process

The data capture process is composed of three distinct phases: the *crawling* phase, the *parsing* phase, and the *exporting* phase. These phases need to be carried out in chronological order, since results from one phase are used as inputs for the next step. Figure 5 illustrates the three phases as well as the resources that are used during the data collection process. The process of data capture involves raw data pulled from *Facebook*, data handling and processing using *PHP scripts* (PHP: Hypertext Preprocessor), and data storage and retrieval using a relational *data base*. Finally, the export files are further processed in the *Stata* software package. This final step is described in the following section on data curation.

Crawling phase: The data source, the directory and application page, is highly dynamic and changes constantly. This poses a challenge because historic data is lost if it is not preserved in some way. The objective of the crawling phase is to discover and permanently store what would otherwise be lost data. For this purpose, a set of PHP scripts (the "crawler") was developed shortly after the public launch of Facebook's platform for applications in May 2007. The crawler automatically browses the application directory and attempts to identify all applications contained in it. The crawler also downloads and saves each application page in a separate text file for later analysis. These text files represent the key input for the parsing phase. The crawler started to store application pages on July 2, 2007 and continued until July 2009.

Parsing phase: Facebook provides its application directory and application pages in the form of hyper-text markup language (HTML) documents. HTML is a standardized language that contains structured text along with formatting markup and other elements for the purpose of presentation by the user's browser. The markup allows the identification of the relevant elements of the HTML file. The data is then assigned to specific data fields in a data base. This process is here referred to as parsing and describes the extraction of the desired content from the HTML documents.[36]

Figure 5: Flowchart of process and resources of the data capture process

Note: Graphic illustrates process of capturing the data from the Facebook web site and processing it to a format to be used with the statistical software Stata. The symbols used follow Flowchart-methodology and are defined below.

Source: Keller (2009)

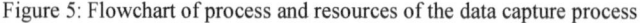

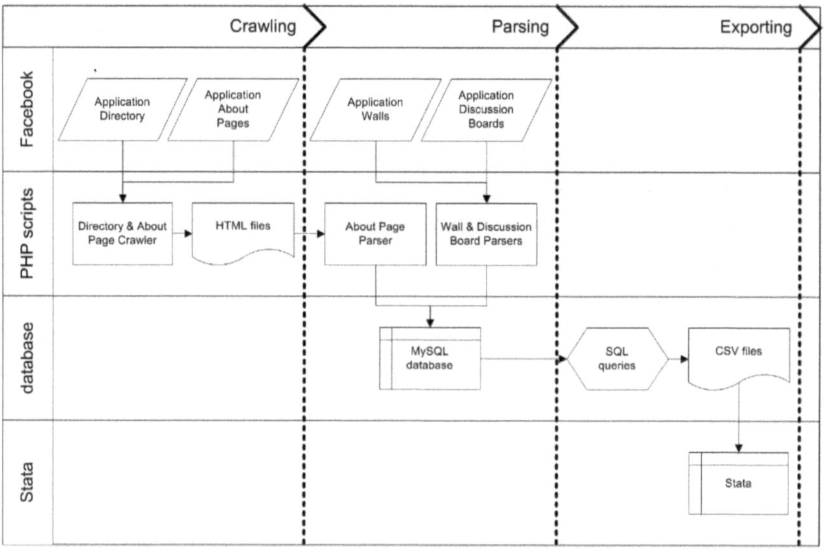

Exporting phase: The goal of the exporting phase is to prepare the content of the data base for later analysis in a statistical software package such as Stata. The data base is an intermediate representation of the gathered data as it structures the data and integrates it in tabular and relational form. However, Stata is not equipped to handle relational links between data base tables. These need to be transformed into strictly tabular data structures. To create these exports, a set of SQL (structured query language) queries is run against the data base. The results are saved into CSV (comma-separated values) files suitable for import in Stata. These export files are described in the following section.

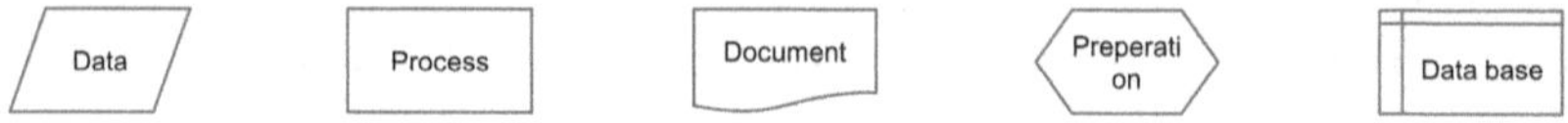

[36] Three separate parsers were written for the application pages as well as for the comments and discussion entries by users. A detailed description of the parsers and the relational data base schema are available from the author upon request.

2.3.2 Export file

This section introduces the export file and the raw data that was captured by the auto-mated crawler and parser and then saved in a data base. The main export from the data base, hereafter referred to as application export file, consists of daily observations from July 2, 2007 to June 30, 2008. It holds data on application usage metrics, some developer measures, count data on updates, Wall posts as well as an assignment to cat-egories.[37] A detailed description of the data, the variables and first summary statistics are presented in the following section 2.4.1.

When compiling the application export file, the exact timing of entry had to be treated with care. Determining the market entry of most Facebook applications is straightfor-ward. When developers decide to publicly launch their application, they submit it to the application directory. In most cases, the application is approved by Facebook with-in a few days and it appears in the list of "newest" applications. This event is consid-ered the market entry of the application. The data set directly reflects the time of this event due to the daily execution of the directory crawler that downloads and stores the application pages of all applications it finds in the directory.

Later, the application page parser transforms each of these stored pages into an obser-vation in the data base. The date of the earliest of these observations is the best esti-mate for the time of entry of most applications in the data set. However, the delay of six weeks between the launch of the directory and the start of data collection necessi-tates refinement of this general approach. Applications that are observed on the first day of data collection might have been launched exactly on that date or up to six weeks earlier, when the Facebook platform launched publicly. The estimation of the entry date of an application may be improved by analyzing contributions to the appli-cation's Wall or discussion board. Posts that date earlier than the first observation in-dicate that the application was launched prior to the previously determined date. In August 2007, an automated crawler and parser collected the date of all user messages to the Wall or the discussion forums of the application page. The earliest date of these first posts is used to improve the accuracy of the estimated market entry for each ap-plication in the data set. This approach reduces the entry date of applications that launched on or before July 2, 2007, on average by 11.81 days indicating an improved

---

[37] There is a second export file that only contains data that matches applications to developers. This data is needed for the analysis of developer portfolios in chapter 3.5 and chapter 5.

estimate of the market entry for those applications. I tested the accuracy of this approach by also applying it to all applications in the data set. Here, the estimated entry date from the first Wall post is only 0.43 days before the date derived from the first appearance in the directory.

2.4 Data curation

This chapter describes the process of data transformation from the raw export data to a data set which is used for statistical analyses. First, the data is imported in the statistical software package (see 2.4.1). Second, the data is manipulated in several steps that ensure a consistent data set for subsequent empirical studies (see 2.4.2). Besides descriptions of the separate steps of the process, this section also contains first summary statistics of the data.

2.4.1 Data import

The export from the SQL data base produces a number of comma-separated text files that need to be imported and merged for subsequent statistical analysis.[38] During the import stage variables are named, labeled and formatted. The resulting imported data set contains data on 32,543 applications for the time period from July 2, 2007 to June 20, 2008 (i.e. 3,506,562 observations).

Table 1 lists the variables that identify each observation (unique identifiers for applications and dates) as well as 21 variables that capture different application characteristics. The data set contains information on the name and the category that each application was assigned to at a given date. The application data also provides information on the developer who is responsible for the application. Here, the distinction is made between individuals, companies, and Facebook. A developer who puts down his name and identity as a Facebook user on the application page in the directory is defined to be an individual developer. Since more than one individual can be assigned to an application, another variable counts the number of individuals for every given day. On the other hand, developers can also include the name or web site of a company or project on the application page. In this case, the developer is referred to as company developer. Finally, Facebook has its own applications (like a photo slideshow or an event management tool) which are also included in the directory.

---

[38] In this dissertation, the data is prepared with the statistical software package Stata 11 (see Stata Corp.'s website for more information: http://www.stata.com).

Table 1: List of variables of application-centric data set

Variable name	Description
Identifiers	
dayOfObservation	*date*
appId	*Facebook application id*
Name and category	
name	*application name*
cat1	*category 1 of application*
cat2	*category 2 of application*
Developer	
numDevelopers	*number of authors*
developerType	*type of developer (company, individual or Facebook)*
Usage metrics	
numInstallations	*number of installations*
numDailyActiveUsers	*number of daily active users*
percentDailyActiveUsers	*daily active percent of total*
Rating and user interaction	
rating	*average rating*
numFans	*number of fans, total count*
numWallPosts	*number of Wall posts, total count*
numReviews	*number of reviews, total count*
numDiscussionTopics	*number of discussion topics, total count*
firstDayInDirectory	*date of first observation*
firstWallPost	*date of first Wall post, taken from old data base*
Update information	
nameUpdate	*application name was updated (0/1)*
descriptionUpdate	*application description was updated (0/1)*
aboutUpdate	*'About the Developer' text was updated (0/1)*
screenshotUpdate	*application screenshot was updated (0/1)*
developerUpdate	*developer updated (0/1)*
categoryUpdate	*application categories were updated (0/1)*

The data set also includes variables that measure the usage of the applications over time. Facebook at first only reported the number of installations of each application. After around three months, however, Facebook changed the measurement to one that captures the actual usage and engagement of users with the application more directly. Since August 29, 2007, Facebook reports daily active users for each application. Active users are defined by the number of users who "touch" an application on a given day (measured from midnight to midnight each day).[39] The number of total installa-

---

[39] The "touch points" are defined technically by different data base calls. See the developer blog for the announcement and description (Facebook 2007a).

tions can still be derived for each day because Facebook also reports the percentage of active users compared to all users who have installed the application.[40]

Furthermore, the data set includes information on how users rate and discuss each application. While there are measures that count the number of fans, Wall posts, reviews and discussion topics, the rating measure is the daily average of all ratings by users of the application (on a scale of one to five, with five being the best).

Finally, a series of indicator variables measure whether certain elements of the application page in the directory were changed on each given day. Specifically, the data set includes whether changes were made to the application name, its general description text or the description of the developer, the screenshot of the application or the assigned category or developer.

2.4.2 Data manipulation

This section describes all data management tasks performed on the imported data that change (i.e. manipulate) the original imported data set. Data manipulation may include dropping observations, replacing observations, or creating new observations from computing values based on the original data. There are two steps in which these tasks are performed on the data. The application data, which is available on a daily observation basis, is first examined for inconsistencies and whether data should be excluded. I call this step the "cleaning of the daily data set". The second step consists of a "conversion to weekly data". The resulting data set is the basis for additional sampling and the empirical analysis in chapters 3 and 5.

Cleaning of daily data

The data cleaning step is necessary because the dynamic structure of the data source makes automated data collection prone to inconsistencies. Changes to the design of the application page or server outages lead to periods in which the crawler is not able to find and store any or not all application pages in the directory. The resulting missing data and inconsistencies are identified and dealt with in several steps:

---

[40] Note: 1,000 active users (24h) and a percentage of active users of 10% denotes that there are 10,000 installations of the application in total. Of these, 9,000 users (i.e. installations) have not interacted with the application in the previous 24h.

Figure 6: Overall usage of Facebook applications including benchmark for outliers

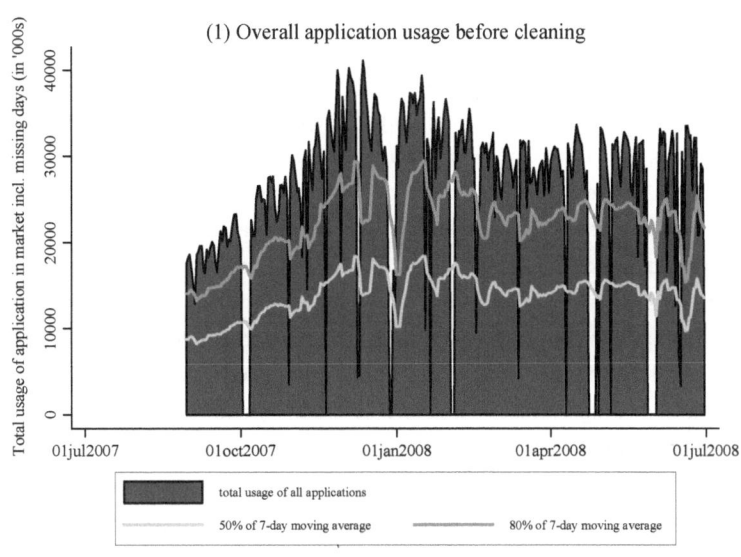

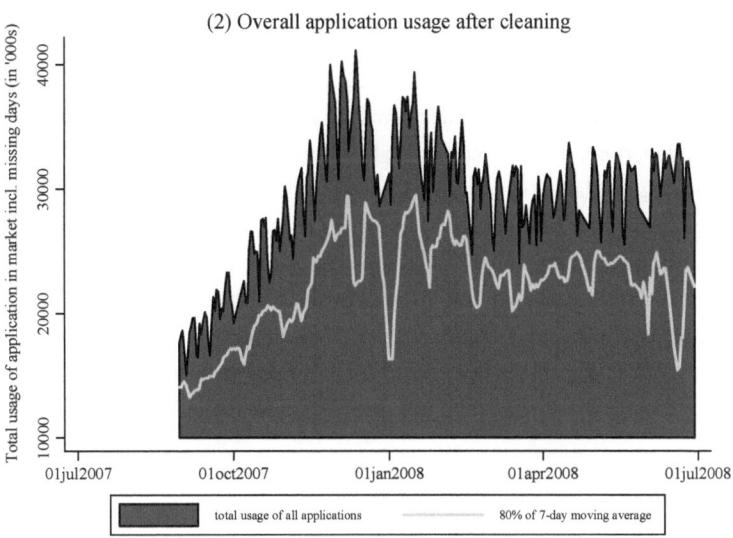

Note: Graph illustrates the missing days and outliers in the data before and after cleaning. In panel 2, 26 days are dropped that were identified as outliers.

1) *Exclusion of applications developed by Facebook*: Facebook maintained 23 applications which were listed in the directory of applications during the time of this study. These applications were excluded from the data because Facebook did not report usage statistics for any of the applications. Examples for applications that were dropped are "Events", "Gifts", "Music Player", "US Politics" and "Photos".

2) *Exclusion of days with outliers in overall application usage*: The overall application usage for each day in the data set is a reliable measure to evaluate whether there are days on which the crawler performed poorly. There are two explanations for such outliers. First, the crawler may have not captured any data on a given day due to, most likely, a server outage. Second, the crawler may have missed applications which constitute a large share of the overall usage of Facebook applications on the platform. In order to follow deterministic criteria to identify days on which the crawler performed poorly, a benchmark for being an "outlier" is needed.

For this, moving averages based on a seven day window as well as fractions of this measure were computed. In panel 1 of Figure 6 the black area denotes the available daily data including zeros for days with no crawler data at all. The two lines plot the 50% and 80% fraction of the seven day moving average of the same data (weekly average of six previous days and the actual day). In the following, I define an outlier day to exhibit overall market usage of below 80% of the seven day moving average. Based on this criterion, 26 days[41] are dropped from the data set. The second panel of Figure 6 plots the data after the exclusion. The area denotes the overall market usage (excluding zeros for missing days) of the clean data set and, for comparison, the line denotes the 80% fraction of moving average based on data including the flawed days.

3) *Exclusion of applications with large gaps in the data*: After excluding the clearly identified outlier days, each application was examined with regard to missing days and gaps in the available data. A missing data day is defined as day in which no data exists for an application. A data gap is any number of consecutive days in which no data is available. For example, if there are four missing data days in a row, the data gap is four. In addition to gaps in the data because of the previous exclusion of

---

[41] The days are: 04sep2007, 29oct2007, 06nov2007, 09nov2007, 29nov2007, 09dec2007, 10dec2007, 27dec2007, 30dec2007, 31dec2007, 18jan2008, 17feb2008, 18feb2008, 28feb2008, 13mar200, 09apr2008, 22may2008, 26may2008, 08jun2008, 13jun2008, 15jun2008, 16jun2008, 18jun2008, 26jun2008, 27jun2008, and 30jun2008.

days, gaps may occur if the crawler did not collect the application page for a given day.

In panel 1 of Figure 7, I plot the graph of the number of missing days relative to all days in which the application is in the data set. The graph shows that most applications exhibit missing data of between 10% and 22% of all days. The graph also shows that only applications with very low usage exhibit more than 35% missing data days.[42] As a consequence of this observation, I decided to exclude applications which miss more than 50% of the possible data days.

Figure 7: Distribution of gaps in the data by size of application

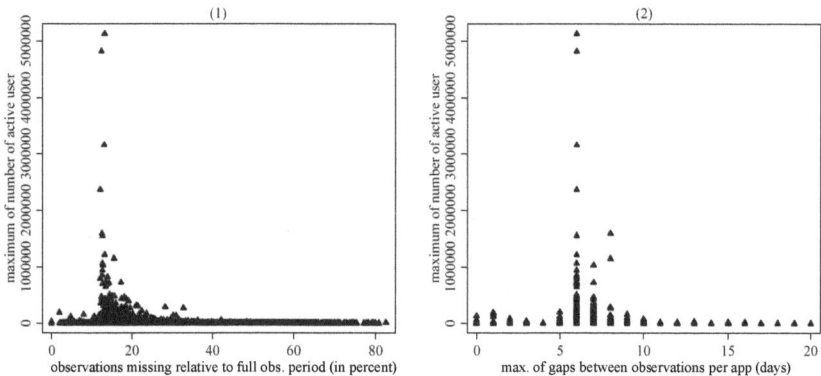

Note: Graph illustrates the distribution of gaps in the data by size of application.

In addition to this first exclusion criterion, I examine the largest gap for each application. Panel 2 of Figure 7 plots the largest (maximum) gap for each application (again by maximum of daily active usage). The graph shows that most applications have a gap of five to eight days at least once in the data. There are applications with gaps of up to 20 weeks as well. Those, however, only have very low active usage. At this stage, I exclude applications which have data gaps of more than 14 days.

---

[42] Note that there are applications that exhibit more than 60% and up to over 80% of missing data days. None of these applications, however, exhibit high usage. In the very most cases, the reason for the high value of missing data days is the short total time that an application is in the data. If an application is in the directory for only five weeks and the crawler misses it in three of these weeks, it misses 60% of the possible days.

4) *Exclusion of applications for the non-English-speaking market*: With the increasing internationalization of Facebook, developers began to build applications in non-English languages. In order to generate a clearly defined market and audience, the applications names were checked in several steps for non-English titles. First, all applications with a maximum of more than 1,000 daily active users were manually examined with regard to whether they had "foreign names" or included symbolic characters (e.g. Hebraic, Greek, Asian characters). Finally and based on identifying characters and strings from the previous manual check, all remaining applications were automatically examined for Turkish and Spanish characters as well as other Umlauts.[43]

5) *Minor, additional changes*: Finally, the preliminary analysis of the variables of the imported data set revealed additional outliers in the data. First, observations were excluded if the percentage of active users was not in the interval of zero to 100. Outliers in this variable are not based on the parser but on the way Facebook computes the value. The outliers can be explained if installations and active usage is measured at different times. If active usage is measured after the number of installations, a rapidly growing application could exhibit more active users than installations and, thus have a percentage of active users of more than 100%. Second, selected applications (each without meaningful total usage) were excluded because the display of their very long application names led to more than 30 name changes within their lifetime. Third, five applications were dropped because the rating variable exhibited values which were not in the interval of zero to five.

After these steps of data cleaning, the resulting data set was converted to weekly data. The procedure is described in the following.

Conversion to weekly data

Because of the frequent missing values and gaps in the data, I decided to convert the daily data set to weekly data. This has the advantage of having a data set with gaps of

---

[43] Turkish and Spanish were the languages that were identified to be most common, aside from English. Exemplary applications names that were identified based on Turkish identifying characters are: Çorum, Silmiş, and Profil Sayacı; for Spanish examples are: ¡VAMOS! Festival and ¿Qué personaje de sailor moon sos?; and for other Umlauts: Österreich Fussball and Vilken ål är du?.

not more than one week without having to decide between and accommodate the implications of additional approaches of imputing missing values.

The data was converted by taking weekly averages (means) for all time-variant and numerical variables. If there were missing values for single days within the week, the average for the available days was computed. For the time-variant indicator variables "developer type" and "category", the value of the first observation (i.e. Monday, if available) is taken for the entire week. The variables that denote updates to different elements of the application page were converted by simply marking an element as "updated" if at least one observation within the week indicated an update. The time-invariant variables for the application identifier and name as well as the developer type were not changed.

After this description of the process of capturing and curating the data, in the following I turn to the first exploratory analyses of the Facebook platform for applications.

3   Descriptive analysis of secondary interdependencies

3.1 Chapter overview

It is the main objective of this dissertation to examine the interdependencies that influence whether and to which extent individuals choose to adopt and use applications. I primarily focus on two questions. First, I study interdependencies between users by analyzing individual-level decisions in the adoption of Facebook applications and how they are influenced by active and passive social influence from their friends (see chapter 4). Second, I focus on information transfers (i.e. interdependencies) that arise between products: users discover and learn about an application because of their discovery or consumption of another application offered by the same developer (see chapter 5).

The two questions concentrate on user-centric forms of interdependencies that may have an influence on market concentration and the structure of Facebook's platform for applications. However, there exist other forms of interdependencies on the platform that take a secondary role but are nonetheless important to consider in order to understand the specific market environment on Facebook's platform. In this chapter 3, I analyze and describe these secondary conditions and interdependencies in detail. The findings prepare the ground for the following multivariate analyses of usage interdependencies between users and between applications. I proceed in four steps.

First, I focus on the data set which was introduced in chapter 2. The data set includes extensive information on the usage of individual applications in the early stages of the platform and over a prolonged period of time (namely until one year after the launch). It encompasses the population of Facebook applications and developers during this period and consists of 52 weeks of data on 19,503 developers, 24,299 applications and 33,332 developer-application-pairs (a total of 612,673 observations). This makes it a unique basis for the analysis of interdependencies in the adoption and usage of applications. However, this base data set needs to be examined and reduced. For this I imposed four conditions to ensure that consistent data is available for all analyses. Also outliers, which may distort the analyses, are excluded from the data. I describe the different steps in which the data is sampled in section 3.2. After the sampling process, the data set includes 2,659 developers, 2,670 applications and 3,567 developer-application pairs for the time period of 43 weeks (a total of 94,239 observations).

Next, I examine the market for applications in more detail (section 3.2). Here, based on the above described sample, I analyze and describe the aggregate supply of and demand for applications as well as individual application and developer statistics. The analysis of the aggregate supply and usage of applications shows that there are distinct phases in the development of the market for Facebook applications. While supply increased at a steady rate throughout the sample period (except the sample-related stop at the end of March 2008), the adoption and usage of applications follows a different pattern. From September 2007 until Christmas the same year, the number of installations and also active users increases steadily and rapidly. Demand for applications then levels off and stays constant until the end of the sample period.[44] The descriptive analysis of this section also shows that application and developer success (in terms of application usage) is highly skewed and that the market for applications is highly concentrated. This finding is the basis for the following analyses in chapters 4 and 5. Here I examine whether specific interdependencies between users and applications respectively contribute to this skewed distribution of success.

After this more general description of the market for applications, I focus on an interdependence that arises from the structure of the Facebook Platform. With the steady increase of software platforms (Evans et al. 2006) such as Facebook, it becomes increasingly important for operators of these platforms to manage third-parties and evolving markets and eco-systems. Here, mechanisms go much further than price setting (Boudreau & Hagiu 2010). In the case of Facebook, setting rules and restrictions for the developers of applications, influences how the users consume the service. In section 3.4, I focus on a particular period during which Facebook changed the way developers could address their users and how notifications about application usage were displayed on user profiles. It is important to examine this case because it shows how interdependencies between users (which are analyzed in chapter 4) are influenced by the decisions of a third-party, here Facebook as platform operator.

Finally, I shift the attention to the management of applications and examine interdependencies within the portfolio of one developer. In section 3.5, I discuss different forms of interdependencies such as potential learning effects or usage effects and whether they motivate developers to build more than one application (i.e. a portfolio of applications). The main part of this section consists of the analysis of a specific inter-

---

[44] Potential causes for this particular development are discussed in the following section 3.3 that analyzes the impact of a Facebook policy change on application usage.

dependence within a developer's portfolio: the time that elapses between application launches. This question is of relevance because it provides insights into the decision making of developers and whether the launch of a new application is influenced by the previous application's success or growth path as well as other developer or market characteristics. One of the findings is that the previous application's success does not have a significant impact on the timing of the next application's launch. This result is important since it has consequences for the choice of empirical methodology that is used in order to analyze the primary interdependence between applications: the spillovers of usage (see analysis in chapter 5).

The chapter closes with a summary and conclusion in section 3.6.

3.2 Sample

The data set described in chapter 2 is the full population of applications and developers on Facebook's platform from its launch in May 2007 (respectively July 2007 when the crawler captured the first data) to June 2008. The following analyses are not performed on this full data set. Rather, a number of conditions are applied that applications and developers need to fulfill in order to be included in the base sample. The conditions are chosen in order to ensure that consistent data is available for all analyses and that outliers, which may distort the analyses, are excluded from the data.

The sample selection process consists of four steps.[45] In Table 2, I summarize the number of developers, applications and developer-application-pairs which were dropped at each stage:

1. **Application entry time**: Applications that were launched before September 2, 2007 and after March 31, 2008 were excluded from the sample. I impose this condition on the sample since data on daily active usage is first available for a full week for the week starting September 2, 2007.[46] Since I am examining entry events and usage in the first weeks after entry, this data is critical to the later analyses. Furthermore, the exclusion of applications that were launched after March 31, 2008 ensures that there are three months of usage data available for

---

[45] The extensive documentation in form of do-files of the sample selection is available from the author upon request.

[46] Of 24,299 unique applications in the data set, 3,386 (13.93%) entered before September 2, 2007 and were dropped.

all applications.[47] After this sampling step, there are 10,660 developers and 13,623 unique applications in the data set.

2. **Availability of data on developer-application-pairs**: Some of the subsequent analyses are based on the research unit "developer-application-pair". This identifier is important because of two reasons. First, the structure in which individuals are affiliated with applications is dynamically changing. Individuals may be developers from the start and leave this role after a while or join a developer team later in the application's life-cycle. Second, multiple individuals may be affiliated as developers of an application at the same time. I excluded developer-application-pairs for which less than 12 weeks of data exist.[48] This assures that sufficient data for the following analyses are available for each unique pair. Note that this does not necessarily entail that a specific developer or application is excluded from the sample entirely. Only the unique affiliation of a developer with an application is too short to meet the condition for a developer to be included with this specific application in the sample.[49]

3. **Relevance of application usage**: The distribution of active usage of Facebook applications is very strongly skewed: few applications make up for the vast majority of usage and most applications never reach a meaningful user base. While the research question, which applications succeed or fail, is an interesting and important one, it is not the focus of this dissertation.[50] As a consequence, applications are excluded from the sample if they do not meet a simple test on relevance. For this sample, I chose the arbitrary number of 100 daily active users. If an application does not reach this usage at least once on a weekly average, it is

---

[47] Of 24,299 applications in the data set, 7,290 (30.00%) entered after March 31, 2008 and were dropped.

[48] After the first sampling step, there are 19,238 unique developer-application-pairs in the data set. Of these pairs, 5,587 (29.04%) do not meet the requirement of the second sampling step and are excluded.

[49] Note: additional observations could be kept if developer information is extrapolated after the week (2008w8) in which developer information stopped being obligatory on application About-pages. However, this would require additional assumptions on the affiliation of developers with applications. As a consequence, a more restrictive approach was taken in this dissertation.

[50] Understanding the success factors of applications is a difficult task. For example, Onnela & Reed-Tsochas (2010) observe in their study of Facebook applications that applications benefitting from a "spontaneous emergence of social influence" between Facebook users are propelled to extraordinary levels of popularity.

dropped from the data set.[51] The combined total usage of the dropped applications amounts to 2.34 million users. The overall usage of all applications in the data set was 839.97 million users. The dropped applications, thus, only account for 0.28% of the total usage and consequently can be assumed to be irrelevant.[52] I conclude that running analyses based on this sample captures the effect for the vast majority user interactions with Facebook applications.

4. **Multiple launches in same week**: Finally, applications are excluded if a developer launched or was first affiliated with them in the same week. This exclusion is necessary since I study the impact that the entry of applications in the market has on previous applications. For this analysis a sequential and unique ordering of applications by developer is critical. In order to achieve this unique ordering, all applications but one were dropped from the sample if their first appearance in a developer's portfolio fell in the same calendar week.[53] The decision which application to keep was made based on a non-random criterion: the application with the largest maximum weekly average of active usage.[54]

These four sampling steps reduced the data set considerably (see Table 2). The base data set described in chapter 2 consisted of 52 weeks of data on 19,503 developers, 24,299 unique applications and 33,332 unique developer-application-pairs (a total of 612,673 observations). The sample after the four stages of reduction includes 2,659 developers, 2,670 applications and 3,567 developer-application pairs for 43 weeks (a total of 94,239 observations).

---

[51] After the second sampling step, there are 10,837 applications in the data set. Of these applications, 7,270 (67.08%) do not meet the requirement of the third sampling step and are excluded.

[52] A different, also arbitrary, choice of minimum active usage would be 1,000 daily active users. There are 1,265 applications that reached that amount of usage at least once (the share of the overall usage of these applications is 1.76%). Due to the significantly lower number of applications for the resulting sample, I chose to only drop applications with under 100 active users as maximum usage.

[53] After the third sampling step, there are 4,757 unique developer-application-pairs in the data set. Of these pairs, 1,190 (24.91%) are multiple releases per day as defined by the fourth sampling condition. They were dropped from the data set.

[54] A potential improvement, particularly because it would increase the number of research units, would be a data set that includes multiple cases for the respective transition which could be controlled for via indicator variables in the estimation. However, this approach brings new and different questions of how to define the sequential order of all applications. As a consequence, the above described approach was chosen for this dissertation.

Table 2: Overview of sample reduction[55]

		devs	apps	dev-app-pairs	obs.	reduction (in %)
Full data set		**19,503**	**24,299**	**33,332**	**612,673**	
Sampling step 1: application entry	*dropped*	8,843	10,676	14,094	230,639	37.64%
	after	10,660	13,623	19,238	382,034	
Sampling step 2: at least than 12 weeks data	*dropped*	2,442	2,786	5,587	26,795	7.01%
	after	8,218	10,837	13,651	355,239	
Sampling step 3: relevance of application usage	*dropped*	5,557	7,270	8,894	231,596	65.19%
	after	2,661	3,567	4,757	123,643	
Sampling step 4: multiple launches per week	*dropped*	2	897	1,190	29,404	23.78%
	after	2,659	2,670	3,567	94,239	
Sampled data set		**2,659**	**2,670**	**3,567**	**94,239**	**84.62%**

This means that the original data set was reduced by about 85% in terms of observations that were dropped from the data set. The reductions of step one and two are necessary in order to have consistent data for every application and developer. However, there is no apparent bias resulting from this selection because it is a definition of the period on which the study focuses. In the interpretation of the results of the following analyses one nevertheless needs to consider that the findings relate to this period. The largest reduction results from excluding applications with very low usage. However, the reduction by more about 65% in terms of observations only decreased the total usage of application in the data set by less than 0.5% - leaving the vast majority of meaningful (in terms of usage) applications in the sample. This is a first indication that success of applications (in terms of application usage) is highly skewed and concentrated among few applications.

The following analyses are based on this sample. If additional restrictions and reductions are necessary, I describe them in the respective chapter.

---

[55] In the table, I abbreviate as follows: developers (devs), applications (apps), developer-application-pairs (dev-app-pairs), and observations (obs).

3.3   Description of the Facebook platform for applications

This chapter describes the Facebook platform for applications. It contains an overview of the supply of and the demand for applications on the aggregated platform-level (section 3.3.1). Furthermore, it summarizes the usage both on the application and the developer level (section 3.3.2).

3.3.1   Aggregated supply and demand

An analysis of aggregated statistics of Facebook's platform for applications entails an analysis of two market sides: (1) the number of applications that are supplied by third-party developers and (2) the number of applications that users of the Facebook service and platform install and actively use during the sample period. Both are described in the following.

Facebook Platform was immediately well and almost euphorically received in the developer community. The launch of the platform was staged as a major event for about 750 developers and media correspondents in which CEO Mark Zuckerberg presented the technical interfaces and commercialization opportunities.[56] The event created early buzz, particularly since Facebook was the first major social network service with extensive programming interfaces that third-party developers were able to develop against. Facebook was particularly heralded for its unprecedented openness and access for third-party developers (Arrington 2007).

The platform launched with 65 developer partners who had access to the API and toolkit before the official announcement. Partners included major software and internet companies such as Microsoft and Amazon.com, media outlets like the Washington Post as well as small game developers like RockYou and Slide. The developer partners contributed 85 applications that were available to users from the first day (Facebook 2007b). Success stories of early entrants to the market further contributed to the enthusiasm and within weeks, thousands of developers had signed-up for an account and built and launched applications. After this initial success, Facebook Platform sustained the continued increase in developer and application numbers.

The strong growth in the supply of applications is illustrated in the first panel of Figure 8. It plots the number of applications in the sample for the period September 2007 until

---

[56] A video of Mark Zuckerberg's keynote speech in San Francisco on July 24, 2007 can be accessed at Facebook webpage (Facebook 2007e).

June 2008. Since the sample does not contain the applications that entered before September 2, 2007, there are only 70 newly launched applications in the first week. The number of applications on the market increases steadily and reaches 1,000 applications after ten weeks. The peak of 2,400 applications in calendar week 13 in 2008 is a direct consequence of the chosen sampling criteria.[57] Since no additional applications are considered and few applications are taken off the platform the number of applications decreases slowly and steadily after March 31, 2008.

There are three events worth commenting. First, there is a slight but clearly observable decrease in the growth rate of applications in the last weeks of 2007. The most likely explanation is that developers are less active in building and releasing applications during the Winter and Christmas holidays. Second, there is a break in the graph in the fifth calendar week of 2008. The number of applications drops by about 200 applications. The reason for this drop is a change to the application directory pages from which the data is crawled and parsed (Facebook 2008a). The missing applications may be a result of either applications being removed and not showing up in the new application page format or because of technical difficulties of the crawler. However, after the drop the growth rate is consistent with the previous rate. Third, the black vertical line marks calendar week seven in 2008. In this week, Facebook implemented changes to the Facebook platform that had been announced six weeks earlier and which significantly altered the way in which applications were able to send notifications and invitations to Facebook and application users. The importance and effect of this policy change is analyzed and discussed in section 0. For the entry rate of new as well as the total number of applications there is no change that is clearly observable in Figure 8.

---

[57] Note that the number of applications in the full data set continues to grow at a steady rate.

Figure 8: Supply of and demand for applications on the Facebook platform

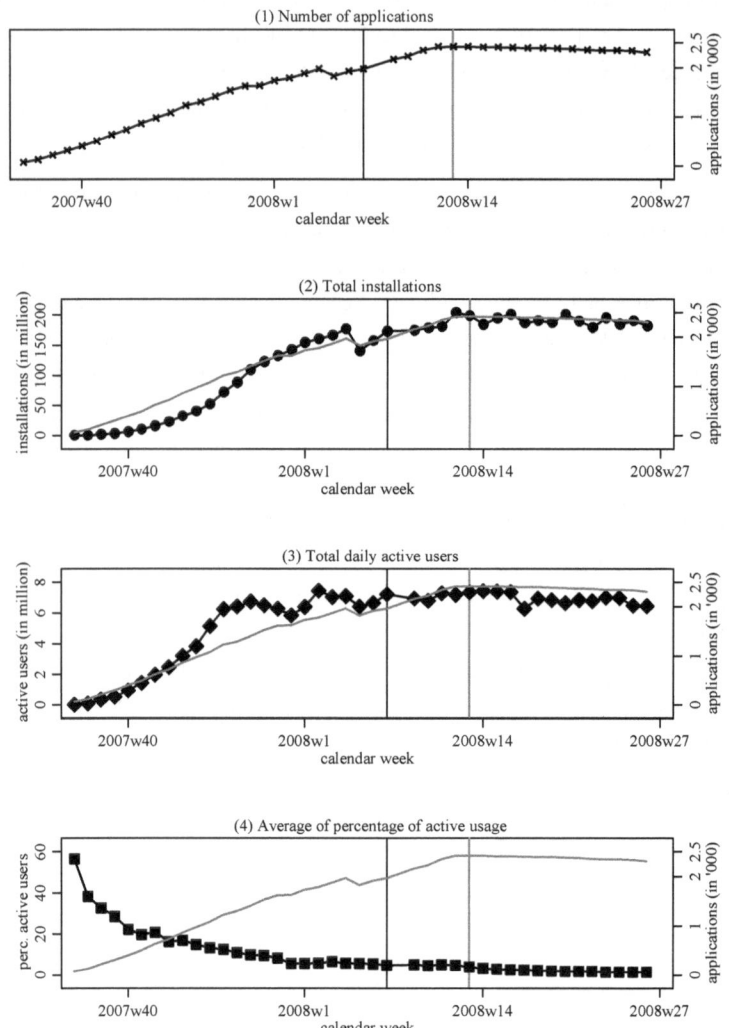

Note: Graphs are based on sampled data. Missing weekly observations due to crawler inconsistencies.
The first vertical line marks the week of the notification policy change, the second line marks the week of last additional application entry.
Panels (2) to (4) include the graph of (1) as a baseline reference.

The adoption and usage pattern by users (demand) of the above-described applications is summarized in the three bottom panels of Figure 8. As a point of reference, the number of applications on the platform is included in all three panels (grey line graph). Panel 2 plots the total number of installations of the applications in the sample. The graph illustrates that the number of installations was also steadily increasing in the sample period – however, at a strongly varying rate. While the first 25 million installations took about eight weeks, the total number increased to more than 125 million in the following eight weeks and reached about 170 million in the fourth week of 2008. The number of installations peaks end of March 2008 – the week before the sample selection excludes additional new applications in the sample (week indicated by the grey vertical line). In the last three months of the sample period, the number of installations stays steady at between 190 to 200 million.

Panel 3 plots the total of daily active users of all applications (average for each week) in the sample. Since there are no or very low costs for users to add and keep an additional application on the profile, users rarely remove an application even if they are not using it anymore. Thus, active usage is a more precise and adequate measure of an application's usage and success. While its growth generally follows a similar path as the number of installations, there are some differences. Most importantly, the daily active usage of all applications in the sample peaks at just below eight million users. This confirms that only a fraction of users who once installed the application and continue to have it on the profile are actively using it. The graph of this percentage of active users (see panel 4 in Figure 8) illustrates this further. Due to higher weight of newly entering applications, the percentage of active users is high in the first weeks of the sample. But as the fraction of new and active applications decreases, this ratio declines steadily towards zero. Another difference is the stronger dip in active usage during Christmas break. This indicates that users not only install less new applications in holidays but also are less actively using existing ones. Also, the increasing disinterest in using existing applications apparently is not compensated by new applications with high absolute usage. Another explanation for the earlier stagnating usage overall may be the more restrictive policies that were introduced early 2008 by Facebook regarding invitations and notifications. A detailed description of these changes is provided in chapter 3.4.2.

The analysis of the aggregate supply and usage of applications shows that there are distinct phases in the development of the market for Facebook applications. While the supply increased at a steady rate throughout the sample period (except the sample-related stop at the end of March 2008), the adoption and usage of applications follows a different pattern. From September 2007 until Christmas the same year, the number of installations and also active users increases steadily and rapidly. Demand for applications then levels off and stays constant until the end of the sample period. There are two explanations for this pattern. First, users generally got increasingly annoyed by the vast and intrusive supply of applications and began to adopt and use applications less eagerly. Second, presumably as a response to user feedback, Facebook implemented a set of measures that changed the way applications interact with users and as a consequence impacted their growth potential. The latter is analyzed in more detail in section 0.

3.3.2   Individual statistics of applications and developers

After analyzing supply and demand in the aggregated platform-level perspective, I now turn to examining the usage of 2,670 unique applications and 2,659 developers.

3.3.2.1   Application usage

I examine the usage of the applications in the sample at different points in their lifetime. Table 3 lists the summary statistics of all applications computed at the week in which each application reached its maximum daily active usage (average for the week). Applications reach their maximum on average after seven weeks on the platform (s.d.: 8). The median is even lower at four weeks and three quarter of the applications reach their maximum usage within nine weeks on the platform.

Table 3: Summary statistics of maximum application usage

N	Mean	SD	P5	P25	Median	P75	P95	Min	Max
max. of active users (by app)									
2670	8709	40016	113	193	519	2279	37685	100	824474
time to maximum daily active usage (in weeks)									
2670	7	8	1	2	4	9	24	1	40

The range of success varies widely. The minimum lies at 100 daily active users – the minimum according to the sampling criteria described in section 3.2. The biggest application in the sample, "Owned!" by the developer Coolapps.com, reached 824,474 active users after 21 weeks on the platform (in the calendar week 23, 2008).[58] At the mean, applications reach 8,709 daily active users in their maximum usage (s.d.:

---

[58] An overview of the 15 largest applications is provided in Table 4.

40,016). The median is significantly lower at 519 users and only a quarter of the applications reach more than 2,279 users in the maximum.[59]

Table 4: List of most successful applications in the sample

Rank	Application name	Application category	Entry week	Max. active usage ('000s)	Time to max. active usage (weeks)
1	*Owned!*	Messaging	2008w3	824	21
2	*Friends For Sale!*	Dating	2007w44	747	33
3	*(Lil) Green Patch*	Education	2007w52	657	27
4	*Pieces of Flair*	Messaging	2007w50	411	29
5	*Mob Wars*	Gaming	2008w4	390	23
6	*Fun Gifts & Events*	Events	2007w38	380	11
7	*Flirtable*	Mobile	2007w47	375	8
8	*Circle of Friends*	Just for Fun	2007w36	367	11
9	*Zoosk*	Just for Fun	2007w52	335	10
10	*Who Has The Biggest Brain?*	Gaming	2007w51	323	28
11	*Best Match!*	Dating	2007w46	307	2
12	*Facebook® for BlackBerry®*	Mobile	2007w43	289	35
13	*PetrolHead*	Just for Fun	2007w40	285	10
14	*Will you KISS me?*	Dating	2007w49	263	8
15	*Sparkey*	Missing	2007w52	256	27

The highly skewed distribution of success is readily illustrated in Figure 9. The top panel plots all applications ranked and sorted by their maximum daily active usage. The graph exhibits the characteristic shape of a long-tail distribution that is typically found in markets for cultural goods such as books and movies as well as software.[60] The distribution of maximum usage of the 100 biggest applications (second panel) follows a similar pattern. The biggest application has twice the usage than the fourth biggest application. The application ranked 25th has a usage of about 190,000 and the 100th of about 52,000 daily active users.

---

[59] I present detailed summary statistics of application usage at different times of the application's time on the platform in Table 22 in the appendix. An analysis of the active usage metrics confirms the above findings. Daily active usage in the mean increases from 3,113 users in the second week and decreases afterwards. Interestingly, in the median, usage peaks already in the second week. The finding that active usage relative to all installations decreases is also confirmed. However, there is some variation in the data. Even after 20 weeks on the platform, 5% of the applications have still more than 7% of their installed base interacting daily with the application.

[60] There is a large body of literature that analyzes the distribution of success in these industries (Brynjolfsson et al. 2003; Brynjolfsson et al. 2006; Anderson 2006).

Figure 9: Market concentration of applications in sample

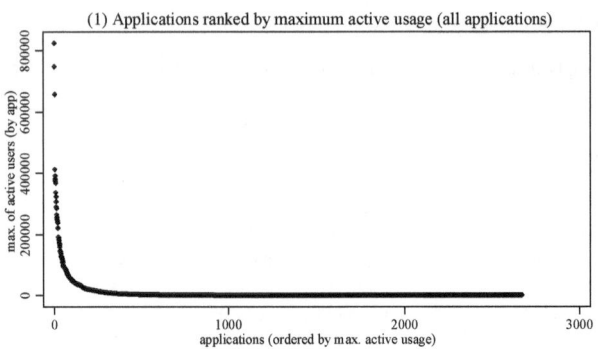

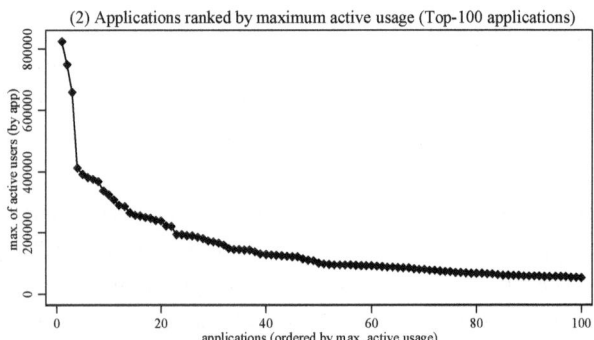

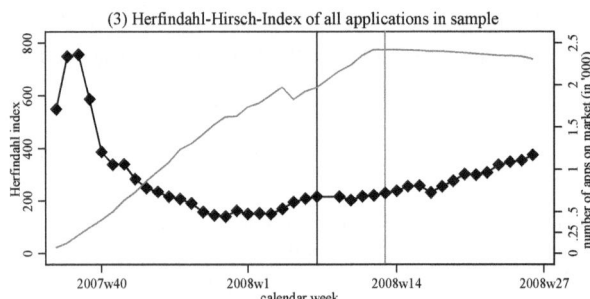

Note: The first vertical line marks the week of the notification policy change, the second line marks the week of last additional application entry.

Source: own calculation.

Note: graphs are based on sampled data.

In a next step, I examine how this strong concentration of maximum success influences overall market concentration in each week. The third panel of Figure 9 plots the Herfindahl-Hirsch-Index (HHI) for all applications for each week in the sample.61 The graph confirms the previous analysis. While the distribution of maximum usage is highly skewed, applications reach their maximum rather early (mean: in week 7; median: in week 4) and their usage as a consequence declines afterwards. With a steady inflow of new applications, market concentration consequently declines. Between September and Christmas 2007 market concentration fell from around 580 to 140 HHI points. This is a significant change in relative terms but the conclusion is that the market, with values below 1,000, is highly fragmented if one examines each week separately. At Christmas and the beginning of 2008, the trend changes and, after it first stays constant at around 160 points, increases slightly in February 2008 when the policy change went into effect (marked by first vertical line).

3.3.2.2 Developer success

This section presents some statistics on the distribution of developer success. The analysis is based on 2,659 developers in the sample.

Table 5: Summary statistics of maximum application usage by developer

N	Mean	SD	P5	P25	Median	P75	P95	Min	Max
max. of active users (by developer)									
2659	10940	48997	105	185	540	2476	42168	1	824494
time to developer's maximum active usage (in weeks)									
2659	9	10	1	2	6	13	31	1	52

Table 5 lists the summary statistics of the maximum application usage by developer. The measure is computed weekly and reports the sum of average daily active usage of all applications that are affiliated with a developer in that week. On average, developers have 10,940 daily active users in the maximum (s.d.: 48,997) and reach that peak after nine weeks on the platform (s.d.: 10 weeks). This exceeds the corresponding value for applications by about 2,200 users. However, when compared at the median, developers only have slightly more users (540 versus 519 users). This may be interpreted in two ways. Either developers with more than one application only have one hit overall or at least not at the same time. For example, Coolapps.com, the developer of

---

[61] The HHI was calculated as the sum of the squared market shares in percent.

"Owned!" (i.e. the largest application in the sample) has additional applications. However, its maximum overall usage is only 20 users higher than the maximum usage of "Owned!".[62]

Analogue to the application success, the first two panels of Figure 10 show that the distribution of developer success is highly skewed. Furthermore, the market concentration, measured by the Herfindahl-Index (see third panel of Figure 10), follows the same pattern as previously observed with applications: it decreases over time and increases after the policy change takes effect. There is a noteworthy spike which breaks the steady decline in November 2007. While I have no definitive explanation for this spike, the most likely cause is that a developer launched a hugely popular application that took a disproportionately large share of the market at that time. After a peak in usage of that application, overall market concentration returned to the predominant trend.

Finally, if one examines the top 25 developers based on maximum usage of all applications (see Table 6), it is interesting to note that there are five teams with a total of 14 affiliated team members that dominate the list. This indicates that the classification of company vs. non-company developer may not be a precise one.[63] Teams and individuals that manage applications with more than 500,000 daily users must operate professional and in some form of incorporated structure. As a consequence, this indicator should rather be interpreted as a branding or marketing decision towards Facebook users. Instead of declaring a website or company as the source of the application, developers opt for the more informal approach of providing individual users or teams as a face to the company.

---

[62] Detailed summary statistics of developer success are presented in Table 23 in the appendix.

[63] See section 2.4.1 for the distinction between individual and company developers. Applications developed by Facebook are excluded from the sample.

Figure 10: Market concentration of developers in sample

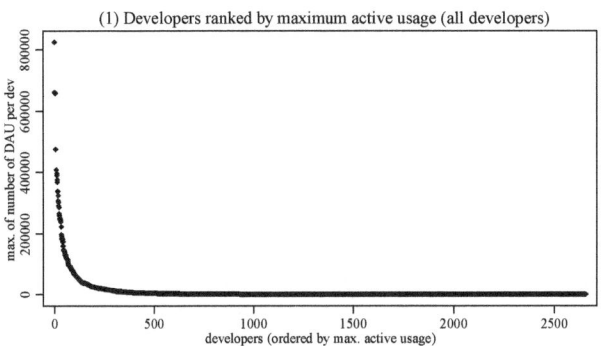

(1) Developers ranked by maximum active usage (all developers)

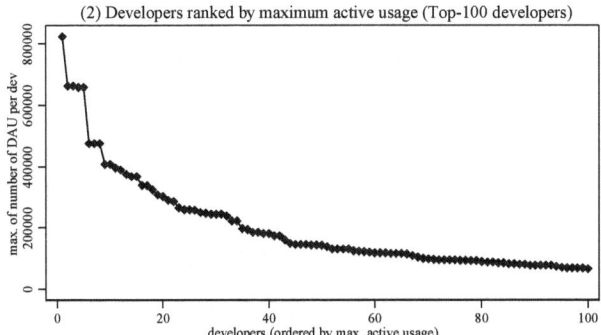

(2) Developers ranked by maximum active usage (Top-100 developers)

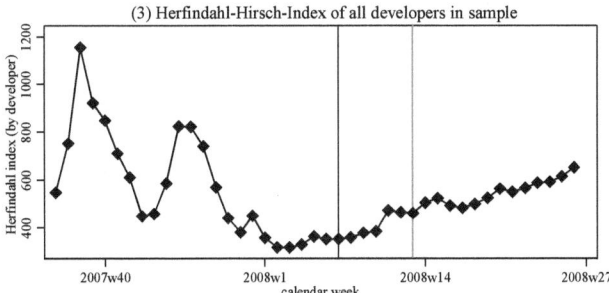

(3) Herfindahl-Hirsch-Index of all developers in sample

Note: The first vertical line marks the week of the notification policy change, the second line marksthe week of last additional application entry.

Source: own calculation.

Note: graphs are based on sampled data.

Table 6: List of most successful developers in the sample

Rank	Developer name	Developer type	Application name (exempl.)	Max. portfolio usage (in '000s)
1	Coolapps.com	company	Trick or Treat	824
2	Alexander Le	individual	Friends For Sale!	661
3	Siqi Chen	individual	Friends For Sale!	661
4	Ashish Dixit	individual	(Lil) Green Patch	657
5	David King	individual	(Lil) Green Patch	657
6	Robby Campano	individual	My Fab Bag	474
7	Davy Campano	individual	My Fab Bag	474
8	David Livingston Kirby	individual	My Fab Bag	474
9	David Mok	individual	Pizza Party	406
10	Ange Low	individual	Pizza Party	406
11	Chainn Inc.	company	Social Profile	394
12	Nirupama Bala	individual	(Lil) Green Patch	389
13	Frengo	company	Flirtable	375
14	Ephraim Luft	individual	Circle of Friends	367
15	Mike Greenfield	individual	Circle of Friends	367
16	Jason Gilbert	individual	Mob Wars	338
17	Zoosk	company	Zoosk	335
18	Playfish	company	Who Has The Biggest Brain?	323
19	grebooca	company	Perfect Match	307
20	Greg Thomson	individual	Jack O'Lantern	300
21	Research in Motion, Ltd.	company	Facebook® for BlackBerry®	289
22	Team Moulin	company	PetrolHead	285
23	Platform Software Inc.,	company	Will you KISS me?	263
24	David Hu	individual	Flying Gifts	258
25	Patrick Lo	individual	Flying Gifts	258

3.4 Analysis of the impact of a policy change on application usage

3.4.1 Introduction

Access restrictions, rules and dynamics of the platform and particularly the market for applications are managed by Facebook with the aim of optimizing its benefit. Facebook's interventions, however, differ from the more common price-setting regulations set by platform operators (Parker & Van Alstyne 2005; Rochet & Tirole 2006). Only recently, research has begun to consider regulatory tactics beyond price-setting such as imposing rules and constraints, creating incentives and otherwise shaping behavior (Boudreau & Hagiu 2010). Facebook disposes of a set of instruments with which it directly and indirectly influences the number and quality of available applications. On the one hand, Facebook can make decisions regarding the technology of the programming platform or the design of the user interface. On the other hand, it forces developers and users to comply with legal terms and conditions that regulate the extent to which developers can use the technological platform and how they can market their application.

Facebook has been actively managing their platform from the start. The following section discusses which dimensions and to which extent Facebook changed the policies for developers and users during this first year of the platform. Section 3.4.3 contains a first exploratory analysis of the impact of Facebook's changes on application usage.

3.4.2 Facebook's changes to platform policies

This section describes three areas in which Facebook acts as private regulator Boudreau & Hagiu (2010) of the application platform that is controlled by the company. First, Facebook set up the platform in a way that allows application developers to monetize usage of their applications. The second refers to Facebook's role in regulating application entry. Most importantly for this dissertation, I examine the rules and changes regarding the developer's opportunities to contact users to adopt and more actively use their applications.

Regulating monetization opportunities

When Facebook launched its platform for third-parties in May 2007, developers may have been primarily intrigued by the opportunities to integrate their applications in Facebook's service. However, there was also a clear economic opportunity. Facebook announced that it would allow "mass distribution" and create "new opportunity (…) to build a business" (Facebook 2007a).

Facebook's objectives are largely aligned with the third-party developers' ones. Both set out to capitalize on a large and active user base. Revenues are realized via selling advertising space to brands, advertisers or Facebook applications that target specific users. Facebook has also experimented with "Engagement Ads" that not only display brand messages but also allow users to interact with a brand through gift-giving, commenting and promotion. Next to each application's canvas page (the space allocated to an application), Facebook can place its own advertising. As a consequence, the more users engage with applications, the more page impressions or time Facebook is able to sell to advertisers. Another strategy is to keep a revenue share of transactions that take place on the platform or by re-directing users to shopping sites (e.g. a music application may forward interested users to the iTunes service where copyrighted music can be purchased). In 2010, Facebook launched its own payment system "Facebook Credits, a virtual currency which can be purchased "pre-paid" from Facebook (Facebook 2011a). This allows Facebook to directly benefit from purchases that go through its system (it keeps a revenue share of 30%). This implies that the level of potential revenue increases with the number of active users of the platform and the applications. Thus, growing the platform both in terms of applications and users is among Facebook's most important objectives.

Application developers are free to monetize their application pages through advertising or other transactions that they control themselves and Facebook deliberately did not impose restrictions on the form of advertising. Advertisements next to the website's content and core functionality are most commonly employed strategy. Here, the placement is determined by the fit between the application's content and the advertiser's message as well as competitive bidding between advertisers (Evans 2008). Similar to Facebook itself, applications can also keep a share of revenues generated by on-site transactions (e.g. online games can offer additional functionality for a premium fee) or by transactions referred to external sites. As an important strategic decision, Facebook decided not to take a share of transaction sales initially, leaving developers to capitalize on this revenue stream.[64]

Regulating application entry

As in most markets with indirect network effects, platform operators want to encourage a wide variety of applications and experimentation in parallel (Church & Gandal 1992; Boudreau et al. 2008). Consequently, they provide developers with a set of tools that decrease their development costs and, thus entry barriers. Low barriers to entry lead to high rates of entry - both from new entrants as well as from developers with multiple applications. This affects both the users' and the developers' utility. On the one hand, a large variety of applications presents novel challenges for consumers to discover and adopt applications (Oestreicher-Singer & Sundararajan 2008; Hervas-Drane 2009). On the other hand, high rates of entry could result in particularly high levels of competition, which again would diminish profits and incentives around the platform (Boudreau 2008b).

It is very likely that Facebook early on planned to facilitate entry of as many developers as possible. The company offered strategic subsidies to third-party developers (Shapiro & Varian 1999) by providing open and well-documented application programming interfaces, multiple development languages, free test facilities, as well as support for developers through developer forums and conferences.[65] Facebook also imposed minimal requirements for applications to be included in the official directory and it does not "police" developers imitating or producing "copy-cats" of existing applications.

Regulating application adoption and usage

For the subsequent analyses of interdependencies between users as well as applications, it is most important to discuss regulatory activities by Facebook that determine

---

[64] Due to the (open) installation process and the lack of a payment system, Facebook could not take a revenue-cut from developers without further development. In contrast, Apple takes a 30% revenue share from all sales in its iTunes store.

[65] Facebook also started a partnership with the server hosting company Joyent (Joyent 2011). The agreement gave Facebook developers a limited number of free accounts and one year of free hosting. This allows developers to focus on building and marketing the applications without having to worry about infrastructure and scalability.

the visibility of applications within the social networking service and have, thus, the most direct affect on its user base.

Users adopt applications through two main channels. First, users of an application can directly invite friends who are not currently users of the application ("invites"). Second, Facebook users get regular updates on friends' activities from the built-in News Feed. To some extent, applications can send messages to this News Feed and signal a friend's activity in this particular application (notifications).[66]

Both channels are regulated heavily by Facebook. In the first phase, from launch in May to August 2007, invites and notifications could be sent almost without restrictions. Application developers used this to "spam" many of their users' friends (Facebook 2007c). Just before September 2007, the start of the sample period, Facebook imposed a set of restrictions and limited the number of invites and notifications per user (Facebook 2007a). In the following months the rules largely remained unchanged.[67]

However, after months of steady growth, Facebook made a series of announcements that changed significantly how developers could utilize both channels. On January 1st, 2008, Facebook announced that it began blocking links in the News Feed, notifications and e-mails, which lead to the installation of applications other than the one whose communication channels were being used. This had an impact particularly on developers with multiple applications and who used existing relationships with users to push out new applications (Facebook 2008b).

On January 10th, Facebook informed developers that users would be offered a "profile clean-up" tool, which would give users the option to uninstall and move applications that are not used frequently (Facebook 2008c). On February 6th, 2008 a major announcement followed that specified that the rules would be changed such that notifications and invites would be allocated based on user feedback. Applications whose users respond more frequently to the notifications/invites that are sent out (a measure for relevance of the notifications/invites), would be able to send out more notifications/invites. One week later, the policy of feedback allocation was launched for noti-

---

[66] See chapter 4 for an empirical study on the influence of these channels on the user's adoption decision.

[67] There was only one change to the way applications were able to send news to a user's feed. Facebook expected that this change might affect growth of applications positively but that it would also lead to higher competition for spots on the News Feed (Facebook 2007g).

fications, requests, and invites. These changes implied that applications that send out more successful notifications and invites could utilize the two channels more actively, leading to a reinforcing loop that favors applications that are used more actively already (Facebook 2008b). In order to enforce these new rules, Facebook also published a set of best practices and information on the escalation of responses that would be taken if the policies were violated (Facebook 2008b). Finally, Facebook announced on February 22, that they would roll out a number of improvements to Facebook profiles that were supposed to simplify the profile and make it more relevant. The team expected that "some challenges could lie ahead for those applications that don't provide value and meaning for users" (Facebook 2008e). Even though the full roll-out did not arrive until mid-July (and thus after the sample period), this announcement is further evidence for the regulatory focus of the Facebook team in early 2008.

What may have motivated Facebook to initiate these changes? And how did it affect application growth and developers? In the early phases of a platform, such as Facebook's market for applications, the platform operator (or regulator) wants to attract entry by application developers. This is done by lowering the costs developers incur when learning the "language" of the new platform. Further, entry can be induced by lowering costs of marketing and ensuring a novel application's diffusion. Hence, Facebook was interested in providing developers with easy access to the option space and awareness of its user base. This was done by allowing developers to send out large numbers of notifications and invites. Highly publicized success stories created a gold rush among developers (e.g. the music application iLike grew to several million users within days). Within weeks, several thousand application developers had signed up for access credentials to the platform and had started to launch a wide variety of applications.

Besides providing specific incentives for developers, Facebook also wanted to "educate" users about the option to install add-on applications to make the service fresh and exciting. Users learned quickly - through invites and a flood of notifications in their News Feed, the vast majority of users had installed at least one application within weeks. Also, many users installed dozens of applications at the same time (multihoming is comparatively costless in the context of Facebook), sometimes even several with largely identical functionality (e.g. within the first month there were several enhanced "Walls" that allowed posting and exchanging of multi-media items). After the initial enthusiasm, however, the sentiment among users towards applications changed. With the rapid increase of the installed base of applications and the increasing professionalization of developers in terms of exploiting the opportunities to use the "viral channels", the volume of notifications and invites grew exponentially. Users were increasingly annoyed by constant updates about their friends' activities and applications. For Facebook (as the platform operator) and the developers this would eventually lead to adverse effects. Instead of inducing additional application adoption and usage, users would start ignoring and delete notifications and requests.

3.4.3 Analysis and discussion

This section contains a preliminary analysis of the impact of the above described policy change on the usage of applications. It also briefly introduces the findings of a related study by Claussen et al. (2010). Finally, it discusses the findings and draws conclusions for the following empirical analyses.

Descriptive analysis of the impact of the policy change

The descriptive analysis is based on 2,670 applications of the sample that was introduced in section 3.2. In order to analyze the impact of the policy change on application usage, I separate applications in the sample in two groups. The first group consists of applications that entered before the eighth week in 2008, the week in which the policy change took effect.[68] Applications that entered in the eighth week or later belong to the second group.[69] Table 7 contains the summary statistics as well as the results of t-tests on the difference of means of selected measures of application usage for the two groups.

---

[68] See the previous section 3.4.2 for a description of the sequence of changes that were introduced by Facebook.

[69] Note that with this approach, applications that launched in the eighth and ninth week are assigned to opposite groups even though they share the same market environment for most of their lifetime. I acknowledge the caveat of this exploratory and simplistic distinction between the two groups. However, due to the early peak in the usage of many applications (see section 3.3.2.1), this overlap is only problematic for a small group of applications. An alternative approach would separate applications in three groups. One group would be constructed applications that completed, for example, eight weeks before the period in which the policy change took effect. A second group would consist of applications that were active for the same period of time but only after the policy change. The last group could be limited to applications that were only active in the time period in which the changes were being announced and introduced (January and February 2008).

The results show that applications are more successful if they are launched before and not after the policy change. In terms of maximum usage, applications of the first group have 555 (median; mean: 9,832) compared to 394 (median; mean: 3,825) active users of the second group (see (A) in Table 7). The difference is even more distinct when looking at the largest applications in each group. The application at the largest five percent quantile in the first group has about three times more users in the maximum than the equivalent in the second group. This finding is confirmed by the results of the analysis of usage at different times of an application's lifetime (see (B) in Table 7). Applications of the first group are consistently more successful after two, four and twelve weeks respectively.

Applications that launched before, on average not only have more active users in absolute terms than applications launched after the policy change. They are also more actively used in terms of usage intensity, i.e. the proportion of active users to all users who have installed the application. The difference is particularly strong after two weeks on the platform (see (C) in Table 7). The median of percentage active usage is 23% for the first group, compared to 14% of the second group. The difference, however, diminishes and is not statistically different after twelve weeks.

The results of this analysis suggest that applications launched after the policy change were less actively used both in absolute and relative terms. It is, however, important to note that such univariate analysis does not control for many other potential explanatory determinants of application usage and success. An alternative, and quite likely, cause for the difference could be that applications that came to market later faced much stronger competition because the number of applications increased substantially over time.

Table 7: Usage for applications launched before and after the policy change

Variable	N	Mean	SD	P5	P25	Median	P75	P95	Min	Max	Sign. Diff.
(A) maximum active usage											
max. of active users											
Before	2171	9832	43549	114	195	555	2609	41610	100	824474	***
After	499	3825	16989	109	171	394	1135	13381	100	249815	
time to maximum daily active usage (in weeks)											
Before	2171	7	8	1	2	4	9	26	1	40	***
After	499	6	5	1	2	4	8	17	1	20	
(B) daily active usage at											
week 2											
Before	2168	3414	16451	20	84	213	891	14159	0	307482	**
After	499	1806	9202	15	71	149	484	5072	1	132020	
week 4											
Before	2168	4286	17892	17	68	202	1090	17876	0	260082	***
After	499	1832	8224	13	56	141	483	9004	1	98188	
week 12											
Before	2168	4134	24940	5	37	127	639	11842	0	528185	***
After	499	1475	6362	6	45	109	369	7218	0	65033	
(C) percent daily active usage at											
week 2											
Before	2168	24	13	6	15	23	32	48	0	94	***
After	499	16	11	2	8	14	23	37	0	57	
week 4											
Before	2168	10	7	2	4	8	12	24	0	58	***
After	499	8	7	1	4	6	11	22	0	47	
week 12											
Before	2168	3	4	0	1	2	4	11	0	41	n.s.
After	499	3	4	0	1	2	4	11	0	37	

Note: The test on inequality is based on two-sided t-tests (*** denotes significance at the 1% level, ** at the 5% level. n.s. denotes "not significant").

Related study on usage intensity of Facebook applications

In a related project, Claussen et al. (2010) examine the effect of the policy change on usage intensity in a multivariate setting. The authors argue that, with the significant shift in incentives for application developers Facebook attempted to increase the average quality of applications and thereby maintain high user involvement and activity.[70]

---

[70] Recall that Facebook implemented a radical policy change regarding the amount of notifications applications could send out: before February 2008, all applications could send out the same amount of messages, while thereafter, the amount of notifications permitted was determined by how frequently the notifications were clicked on, which proxies for applica-

The policy change (assumed to be endogenous to the platform operator but exogenous for application developers) is used to analyze how drivers of usage intensity changed following the policy change. A set of economic determinants that may drive usage intensity is examined: First, network effects from the installed base of an application as well from portfolio effects from applications by the same developer are considered. Second, it is analyzed if and how application age influences usage intensity. Finally, the authors study if the degree of concentration in an application's submarket affects usage.

For a sample of applications, based on the data set from this dissertation, the authors estimate fixed-effect OLS models and analyze the overall effects on an application's usage intensity before disentangling how they are affected by the policy change. The authors find that the policy change led to quantity (as expressed by the number of installations of each application) becoming less important, in line with expectations. Further, they find that applications in more concentrated sub-markets generate higher usage after the policy change, suggesting a move towards winner-takes-all outcomes in such submarkets. Finally, although usage intensity always declines as applications become older, the decline becomes less severe after the policy change, which suggests that the policy change was successful in keeping adopters more active over time.

Conclusions

With the steady increase of software platforms (Evans et al. 2006), it becomes increasingly important for operators of these platforms to manage third-parties and evolving markets and eco-systems. Here, mechanisms go much further than price setting (Boudreau & Hagiu 2010). The above discussed case shows that setting rules and restrictions for one participating party directly influences the other parties. In the early phases of the platform, Facebook put hardly any limitations on how developers implement highly contagious features, which led to exponential growth of some applications. These success stories made the platform attractive for new entrants. However,

---

tion quality. Facebook thus increased incentives for producing high-quality applications and punished applications that send out information considered useless by users.

when the abundance of messages got out of hand, Facebook intervened, crippling developers' distribution opportunities.[71]

The analysis and findings of this section do not allow for a final statement regarding the effect of the policy change. Additional studies that take into consideration various determinants of application success as well as control for evolving market conditions need to be undertaken. The study by Claussen et al. (2010) is a first step. Nevertheless, the description and discussion of the policy change provides a valuable background and basis for the empirical study on interdependencies between users (see chapter 4). The study examines on the individual user level, how different sources of social influence affect the decision to adopt and promote applications. It utilizes survey data which was collected through an online questionnaire in the beginning of February 2008, thus at the end of the "pre-policy-change" period. Since the survey asks respondents to refer to an earlier adoption decision, one can assume that their decision was made at a time in which notifications were published frequently. In such an environment it is particularly interesting to determine the extent to which direct or indirect social influence (see section 1.3.2.1 for a distinction) prevails. The study and its findings are presented in chapter 4.

3.5   Analysis of the time elapsed between application launches

This chapter contains an empirical analysis of interdependencies with developer portfolios. It specifically focuses on the influence of various determinants of the time that developers take between the launches of applications. The chapter is motivated and structured in the following introduction.

3.5.1   Introduction

For the following analysis, I distinguish between two types of developers. A developer holds and manages a portfolio of applications if he developed and launched more than one application (here, by definition, during the time that is covered in this sample). He is hereafter referred to as "portfolio developer".[72]

---

[71] Since this policy change in February 2008, Facebook repeatedly imposed rules on developers. An example is the mandatory use of Facebook Credits as payment system for purchases of virtual goods. Decisions like this have a direct impact on the business of developers.

[72] A developer who only manages only one application (again, by definition, in the time that is covered in this sample) is referred to as "single-app developer".

There are different reasons why developers may choose to build portfolios of applications. After the initial cost of getting acquainted with the Facebook API, the effort of programming and launching the second or next application is significantly lower. Besides learning effects in the development of applications, there are synergies that manifest economies of scale and scope in the management of applications. The second or next application can be run and administered on the same server, marketing expenditures can be synchronized and customer care for several applications can be handled by the same person or team.

Specifically, the potentially positive usage interdependencies between applications in a portfolio are the main research question that is examined in chapter 5. There exists some anecdotal evidence for the points stated above. Established firms with several applications seem to be in a better position to make novel application ideas a commercial success. For example, the social gaming firm Zynga is accused of scouting for popular applications by other developers and studios, creating replicas, and then leveraging its resources in administration and marketing to turn them into hits (Saint 2010). Due to low barriers to imitation in terms of development costs as well as often unspecified protection of intellectual property, these "copy cat" applications are rather common. While some disputes are fought out in court (Arrington 2009), legal action against large firms is often unaffordable for startups or small companies.

On the other hand, developers may choose to focus on one application only, for example if their first application failed in the market place or their experience on Facebook Platform was unsatisfactory in any other way. Reversely, particular success of the first application may also prohibit developers to allocate resources to the development of new applications, if they are caught up with improving the functionality, managing the server load, handling user requests and overall marketing and administrative tasks of a growing business. Anecdotal evidence for this rationale is provided by the case of iLike, an application that allows users to express their music tastes and listen to songs on Facebook. Even though iLike existed as a stand-alone service before the launch of Facebook Platform and the management team consists of experienced specialists, the company was overwhelmed by the scaling issues during the first weeks of its application on Facebook (Eldon 2007).[73] While this describes an example of extraordinary

---

[73] In an interview published on VentureBeat, Ali Partovi, the CEO of iLike, describes how the team was overwhelmed by the early success that required installing more than 100 additional servers during the first weekend.

success, the challenge of scalability of applications and operations was widely experienced and discussed in the developer community (Patel 2007).[74]

Apart from these anecdotal observations in popular publications, there exists neither a conceptual nor an empirical analysis of a representative sample of developer portfolios on Facebook Platform. As a consequence, this section contains two analyses, each of which make a contribution to the scarce research on portfolio management on application platforms. First, an exploratory analysis describes the extent to which developers build portfolios of applications. It also provides a univariate analysis of selected developer characteristics with regard to whether they are single-app or portfolio developers. Second, a multivariate analysis examines the determinants of the time that elapses between application launches of portfolio developers. It considers the influence of different developer characteristics, portfolio success and growth dynamics, market concentration measures and, in an extension, the impact of Facebook's policy change regarding notifications[75]. In addition to these contributions, the results of this analysis have important implications on the choice of research methodology for the analysis of interdependencies between applications. This empirical pre-analysis is suggested by Hendricks & Sorensen (2009) and will be discussed in detail in chapter 5.3.

The analyses of this chapter are based on the data and sample that was described in chapters 2 and 3.2 respectively. The chapter is structured as follows. Section 3.5.2 contains the exploratory analysis of uni-app and portfolio developers. Possible determinants of the elapsed time between applications are discussed in section 3.5.3. It also contains the definition of the variables. The empirical strategy of the multivariate analysis as well as the results are presented and discussed in section 3.5.4. The section closes with a conclusion in 3.5.5.

3.5.2 Descriptive analysis of developer portfolios

As a first step of this exploratory analysis, I examine if developers develop and manage more than one application. In the following, this is measured by the portfolio size which is defined as the maximum of the number of applications that each developer in the sample manages in a certain week between September 1, 2007 and March 31,

---

[74] There were even calls for Facebook to step in and offer services and resources that developers could use or purchase and which would allow smooth interaction and scalability of the third-party applications on the platform (Hendrickson 2007). A Facebook partnership with Joyent offers some of this service (Joyent 2011).
[75] See a description and analysis of this policy change in chapter 0.

2008. Panel 1 of Figure 11, which plots the frequency distribution of the portfolio size for all 2,659 developers, exhibits a highly skewed distribution. 2,207 (83.00%) developers are single-app developers (i.e. their maximum portfolio size during the time of the sample is one). If one only considers the 452 portfolio developers, the distribution is equally skewed (see panel 2). The mean of their portfolio size is 2.99 applications (s.d.: 1.84; median: 2) with a maximum of 15 applications.

Figure 11: Frequency distribution of developers' portfolio size

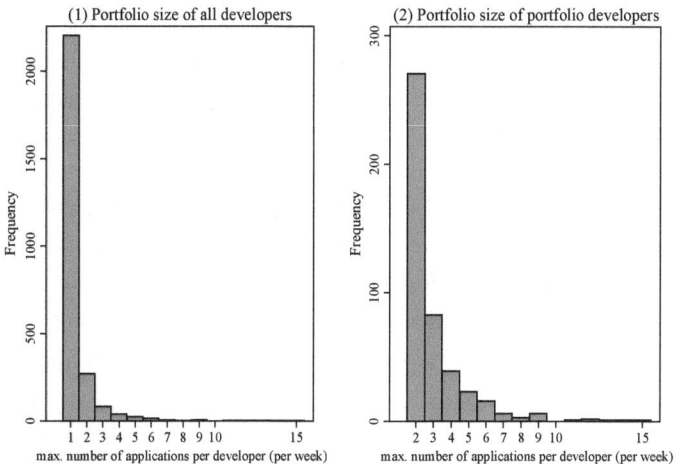

Note: Graphs based on (1) 2,659 developers and (2) 452 portfolio developers.

The main finding is that the vast majority of developers only have one application in their portfolio. Furthermore, if a developer manages a portfolio, it is likely to be small. Only 83 developers (around 18% of portfolio developers) have three applications and 39 developers (around 9%) manage four applications. These results are surprising, particularly in the light of the introductory discussion of the benefits and costs of multiple applications. Without further analysis, however, one needs to be careful about an interpretation.[76]

---

[76] Note that these findings refer to applications that meet the minimum requirement of 100 daily active users in one week of the sample period (see the sample criteria discussed in chapter 3.2). This means that developers may have developed and launched more applications, which, however, did not meet the minimum requirement for relevance. The following

In a second step, I present a set of univariate analyses that examine differences be-tween single-app and multi-app developers. These analyses result in the following findings.[77]

First, there is a significant difference in the share of portfolio developers when consid-ering developers that are listed as a company and those that are not. 11.72% of compa-ny versus 19.92% of non-company developers have more than one application in the sample period and are thus classified as portfolio developer.

Second, portfolio developers have entered Facebook Platform on average in calendar week 42, 2007 and, thus, five weeks before single-app developers have. The difference is statistically highly significant. Three additional tests on out-of-sample measures complement this finding. The share of portfolio developers among developers who entered before September 2007 is twice as high as the share among developers who did not (30.65% vs. 15.02%). Again, the difference is highly significant. Furthermore, portfolio developers have around 122,000 installations compared to the 34,000 instal-lations of single-app developers.[78] Finally, developers who became portfolio develop-ers in the sample period had significantly more applications on the platform before September 2007 (the beginning of the sample period) than single-app developers.

Third, the analysis shows differences in the success developers have during the sample period. In the week with the highest number of daily active users (weekly average), portfolio developers have around 29,000 users (s.d.: 77,004) and thus more than three times more users than single-app developers (mean: 7,184; s.d.: 39,967). In the medi-an, portfolio developers are in fact almost ten times more successful. If one considers the total accumulated usage of all applications by a developer, the results are similar.

---

descriptive statistics were conducted for two additional samples. One contains the portfolio size including "irrelevant" applications for the developers which are included in the sam-ple. Here, the quota of single-app developers decreases to around 60% which indicates that the developers in the sample have indeed developed additional applications that are not considered in the sample. The skewed distribution, however, is unchanged. The other sam-ple contains the portfolio size of all developers before the sampling process. Here, the quo-ta of single-app developers is equally high at around 80% with an equally skewed distribu-tion. Based on these results, the appropriateness of the applied sampling process is support-ed.
[77]

Table 24 in the appendix lists the summary statistics.
[78] The number of installations can be interpreted as the installed base and users that the devel-oper has interacted with at least once before September 2, 2007.

Portfolio developers have on average about 347,000 users in the sample period, whereas single-app developers only have 96,000 users.[79] The distribution of this success metric is again highly skewed. However, in the median, the relative difference between the two developer groups is even stronger with portfolio developers having around twelve times more users. This suggests that additional applications in the portfolio generate significantly more users for the developer overall. If one examines the average success of a portfolio application, however, the difference is not statistically significant. Still, the average application in a developer portfolio is about four times larger in the median than the one application by a single-app developer.

This exploratory analysis brought some first insights in the differences between single-app and portfolio developers. An important finding is that portfolio developers seem to be more successful in the sample period. However, they have, on average, also entered the Facebook platform earlier, thus having more time to develop multiple applications. Furthermore, they were more active developers before the sample period (meaning from May to September 2007). This preliminary analysis, however, does not allow drawing causal conclusions concerning the dynamics and incentives of developers to build application portfolios. Specifically the questions of whether developers are more successful because they have a portfolio of applications or whether they build a portfolio because they had one successful application cannot be answered. This question seems worthwhile for additional theoretical modeling and empirical, multivariate research.

In this dissertation I focus on a specific aspect of these research questions by examining interdependencies between portfolio applications. The above analysis hints that there may be reinforcing processes between applications within a developer portfolio. In a preparation for the subsequent empirical analysis of this question, I study portfolio developers in more detail, specifically regarding the time elapsed between the launch of their applications. Potential determinants of this time as well as their operationalization for analysis are discussed in the following section 3.5.3. The empirical strategy and the results of the multivariate analysis are presented in section 3.5.4. The analysis is based on data on the above described 452 portfolio developers who launched at least two applications in the sample period. These developers have 986 unique applications in their portfolios. Since several of these applications are developed and managed by

---

[79] Note that these are accumulated measures of weekly averages. The actual usage is seven times larger.

more than one individual, there are 1,360 unique developer-application-pairs that will be used as the unit of analysis throughout the following analyses.

3.5.3 Determinants of the time between application launches

After having analyzed differences between portfolio and single-app developers, I examine in more detail the former of the two groups. Specifically, I study what determines the time that elapses between application launches of portfolio developers (hereafter referred to as "elapsed time").

I am not aware of research that examines developer decisions regarding the timing of the launch of an application or specifically the time that elapses between launches of several applications in a portfolio. However, Hendricks & Sorensen (2009) analyze this question in their research on music artists and the release of subsequent albums. The authors argue that the time between releases is a creative process that strongly depends on the "vagaries of the artist's moods and incentives" (Hendricks & Sorensen 2009: 338). They are specifically interested whether the new release depends on the previous album's sales path. For example, artists who spend more time promoting an album will see their current album decline slower but at the same time have less time for writing and producing a new album. For their sample they find that there is no significant relationship between the previous album's sales pattern and the time until the next album's release.[80]

There are arguments that put application markets closer to the music rather than the traditional software market (The Economist 2010). Specifically, it takes on average the same time to write an application as it does to compose a song. As a consequence, I chose to employ a similar methodological approach to analyze the elapsed time between the launch of Facebook applications. However, the reduced model by Hendricks & Sorensen (2009) has been significantly extended by considering additional determinants. There are four categories of determinants that are described in the following.[81]

---

[80] The authors analyze a reduced model that only considers the success and the decline rate as well as category and time controls.

[81] I denote variables that are included in the following empirical analysis with italic script.

Previous application characteristics

Analogue to Hendricks & Sorensen (2009) I am interested in whether different characteristics of the previous application determine the time that elapses to the launch of the following application. First, the previous application's sales path is determined by its success (i.e. the *accumulated usage of its first four weeks*) and the *growth rate* (i.e. the relative change in usage). Second, it is of interest whether there is a substitutive effect between the effort spent on the most recent application and the time it takes to develop the next application. The data on the "About-page" updates approximate this effort and is included via two variables. One counts the *number of updates to the previous application's page* in the two weeks prior to the new application's launch. The second counts the same number for the period of two to four weeks respectively.

Developer characteristics

A second set of determinants relates to developer-specific characteristics. Individuals who develop and market an application either by themselves or as member of a team may put different emphasis on launching multiple applications in a short period of time when compared to companies. This characteristic is included via the indicator variable *company developer*. Furthermore, developers may launch new applications quicker if they are more experienced in conceptualizing, programming and marketing an application. They are also more aware of the overall development of the platform and can cope with changes in the API or user structure more swiftly. I control for this *developer experience* by including a variable that counts the weeks from his first appearance on the platform to the week in which the new application is launched. Additionally, there may be strong experience advantages for developers who joined the platform early and in the turbulent phases of its growth. In order to capture these early entrant effects, I include an *indicator whether a developer was active before September 2, 2007*. I further specify the activity and success of these early entrants by including a measure for the *number of installations that a developer had in the week before September 2, 2007*.

Application characteristics

There may also be differences in the elapsed time between application launches that are specific to certain application characteristics. One of such is the type of application, for example whether it is a social game with comparatively sophisticated functionality versus a short quiz application that is primarily text-based. Also, developers may find it easier to develop or may be incentivized to launch quickly another application that is similar to the previous one. These two effects are captured by including indicator variables for the *category* that the developer assigned the application to as well as an indicator whether the *application was launched in the same category as the previous one*. Elapsed time may also depend on whether the application is one of the first or last in the portfolio. Here, again experience and complementary effects may reduce the time between launches of later applications. This effect is considered by including an indicator variable that denotes whether an application belongs to a certain rank in the application *entry order to the portfolio*. In order to also control out-of-sample effects, a variable on application entry order is computed and included considering all applications in the data set, i.e. also applications that did not meet the minimum requirement of relevant usage.

Market characteristics

Finally, the elapsed time between application launches may depend on the stage of the overall market and Facebook platform. Facebook was in a phase of significant growth and organizational changes during the time that is analyzed in this dissertation. A growing number of applications and competitors shifted the incentives for developers to enter or launch additional applications. Facebook users began to be annoyed by the vast amount of applications and invitations. And Facebook itself altered the competitive environment and the way applications could grow by changes to its policies.[82] In order to account for these changes, I include a *time-dummy* that counts the number of weeks since platform launch. Furthermore, an indicator variable captures whether an application was launched before or after the *policy change* that was made in February 2008. The effect of competition by other applications is included via two measures. One is a count variable of the *total of applications in the sample* for the week in which the application was launched. The other is a measure of *market concentration* (a standard computation of the Herfindahl-Hirsch-Index, HHI). Both measures are also included as *interactions with the indicator for the policy change*.

---

[82] See section 0 for a description and analysis of these changes.

An analysis of these determinants will provide important insights in how developers manage their portfolio. The following section first describes the empirical strategy for the estimation of their effect on the elapsed time between application launches as well as summary statistics of the variables. It then presents and discusses the results and findings.

3.5.4 Multivariate analysis

3.5.4.1 Summary statistics

Before the estimation methodology of the multivariate analysis is presented, this section provides the summary statistics of the variables included in the models. The data consists of 452 developers who launched at least two applications during the study period. The summary statistics are based on 906 "following" applications, i.e. applications that are not the first application of each developer. In the sample, 183 developers launched an additional third and 99 developers an additional fourth application. Only 25 developers (less than 3%) have more than ten applications (see Table 8).

Table 8: Frequency distribution of entry order of application in portfolio

entry order of application in portfolio			
	Freq.	Percent	Cum.
2	452	49.89	49.89
3	183	20.20	70.09
4	99	10.93	81.02
5	62	6.84	87.86
6	37	4.08	91.94
7	21	2.32	94.26
8	15	1.66	95.92
9	12	1.32	97.24
>10	25	2.76	98.01
Total	906	100.00	

First, I describe the summary statistics of the dependent variable: the elapsed time (in weeks) between application launches. On average, 3.89 weeks (s.d. 3.80; median: 2; min.: 1; max.: 22) elapse between the launch of two applications in a developer portfolio. Figure 12 illustrates that the distribution of the variable is highly skewed. For about one third of all applications, the previous application was launched only one week before.[83] This implies that the effort of building and launching an application is very low or that developers build several applications in parallel.[84]

Figure 12: Frequency distribution of elapsed time between application launches

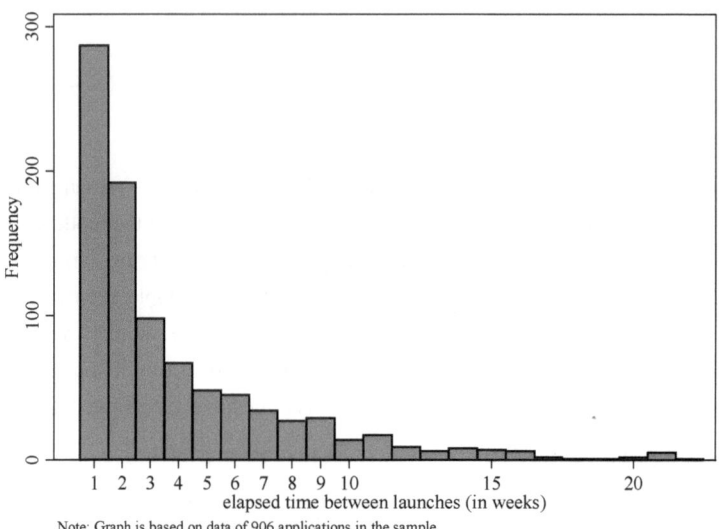

Note: Graph is based on data of 906 applications in the sample.

Table 9 lists the summary statistics of the explanatory variables that are included in the empirical analysis of the elapsed time between application launches.[85] The usage pattern of previous applications of the developer portfolios in the sample is very heterogeneous. The success, here measured in first four weeks accumulated usage, varies widely. Predecessor applications of the applications in the sample on average had 3,000 active users. A median of 23,000 users and maximum of 7.35 million users suggest that the distribution of success is highly skewed. The same holds for the application growth rate. It ranges from a near loss of all usage (see minimum of negative 95% growth) to an immense increase of 14,420%. The reason for these extreme changes

---

[83] There are no meaningful differences in the elapsed time if one considers the entry order of the application separately. The median for each group of applications is between one and three.

[84] The implications for the analysis of spillovers between applications will be discussed in section 5.3.1.

[85] See section 3.5.3 for a discussion of the determinants and description of the variables.

lies in the volatility of usage and the oftentimes low base on which the growth rate is computed.

Another noteworthy feature is the apparently high experience and earlier activity on the platform. Since the study period begins in September 2007, I do not include entries that occurred in the first four months of the platform. However, I control for this activity with different measures. The developers of 32% of the applications in the sample have participated on the platform by launching an application before September 2007. 28% of the applications in the sample are affiliated to developers that are classified as "company developers", indicating that a company or project name was provided instead of individuals' names. Developer success for applications launched before September 2007 again follows a skewed distribution. On average, developers amassed 150,000 installations for these applications (mean; s.d.: 0.67). The median of less than 10,000 as well as a maximum of 6.5 million indicates that few developers managed to win most of the demand for applications. This is consistent with the findings of chapter 3.3 that examines developer and application success in the study period, i.e. after September 2007.

The average application in the sample entered as third application (median; mean: 3.36). The minimum is two because the analysis only considers applications that "follow" on a previous one. Note that the entry order and portfolio size is based on the sample selection criteria specified in section 3.2. If the full portfolio, i.e. including applications that do not meet criteria such as having reached 100 daily active users, is considered, the median of entry order increases to five. The distribution of portfolio size, and hence entry order of applications, is highly skewed. The mean of entry order based on the full sample is at 10.64 and the maximum at 244. This indicates that there are several developers with a very large number of applications. However, none of the developers managed to grow more than 15 applications to a size of at least 100 daily active users.[86]

---

[86] See the maximum of entry order when the sample, as described in 3.2, is considered. This assumes that reaching 100 daily active users on average for at least one week is the strongest selection criteria.

Table 9: Summary statistics for explanatory variables of elapsed time analysis

Variable	Mean	SD	Median	Min	Max
Previous application characteristics					
first 4 weeks accumulated usage (in 100k)	0.23	0.75	0.03	0.00	7.35
growth rate (in percent)	143.05	907.22	3.04	-94.65	14,420
number of updates in previous 2 weeks	1.84	2.33	0.00	0.00	7.00
number of updates in previous weeks 2 to 4	1.81	2.33	0.00	0.00	9.00
Developer characteristics					
company developer (0/1)	0.28			0.00	1.00
experience at application launch (in weeks)	11.38	8.70	9.00	1.00	40.00
entry before Sept 02, 2007 (0/1)	0.32			0.00	1.00
num. installs in week 34, 2007 (in million)	0.15	0.67	0.00	0.00	6.49
num. applications in week 34, 2007	1.00	2.29	0.00	0.00	23.00
Application characteristics					
application in same category as previous (0/1)	0.32			0.00	1.00
entry order	3.36	2.13	3.00	2.00	15.00
entry order (full sample)	10.64	16.53	5.00	2.00	244.00
Market characteristics					
launch after policy change (0/1)	0.17			0.00	1.00
number of applications in launch week (in '00s)	15.11	5.77	16.22	1.24	24.20
policy change interaction: num. apps (in '00s)	3.85	8.40	0.00	0.00	24.20
HHI in application launch week	220.58	102.98	207.94	140.71	754.99
policy change interaction: HHI	37.68	82.06	0.00	0.00	229.22
weeks since platform launch	31.57	7.10	31.00	17.00	47.00

Note: N = 906 applications.

Finally, a number of market characteristics indicate the platform's stage of development in terms of age and competitive environment. Market concentration during the study period varies strongly, namely from 141 to 755 points on the Herfindahl-Hirsch-Index (HHI). Note that standard convention would lead to the interpretation that the market is not concentrated and, thus, highly competitive. The HHI, however, is influenced by the large number of applications with the same, i.e. very low, market share (compare analysis of distribution of success in section 3.3.2). As a consequence, an interpretation in comparative terms seems more appropriate. The summary statistics indicate that market concentration for some applications is more than five times higher than for others at the time of launch.

After this description of the data[87], the following section specifies the model that is used to estimate the elapsed time between application launches.

---

[87] In addition to the descriptive analysis, Table 25 in the appendix contains the correlation table for the variables included in the estimation.

3.5.4.2 Model specification

This section introduces the empirical approach for the multivariate analysis of the time that elapses between the launch of two applications. It includes a description of the estimation methodology and specification of the estimation models.

Estimation methodology

In order to analyze the determinants of the elapsed time between application launches, I employ a simple hazard model where the survival (here, launch of the next application) is considered as a nonnegative random variable T.[88] A basic concept for the analysis of survival times is the hazard function $\lambda(t)$, which is defined as the limit

$$\lambda(t) = \lim_{\Delta t \to 0} \frac{P(t \leq T < t + \Delta t \mid T \geq t)}{\Delta t} \tag{1}$$

and measures the instantaneous failure rate at time t given that the individual survives until t. In the following analysis, survival models are estimated where the hazard function depends on a set of covariates $x' = (x_1, ..., x_p)$ that influence the survival time T.

The Cox's proportional hazard model (Cox 1972) is a common reference model for multivariate survival analysis. Here, the hazard rate is assumed to be the product

$$\lambda(t,x) = \lambda_0(t)\exp(x_1\beta_1 + ... + x_p\beta_p) = \lambda_0(t)\exp(x'\beta). \tag{2}$$

In this model the baseline hazard rate $\lambda_0(t)$ remains unspecified. The covariates x, through the exponential link function, act multiplicatively on the hazard rate. Analogue to (Hendricks & Sorensen 2006; Hendricks & Sorensen 2009), I use a set of time-invariant regressors x_i in the models. The base specification that is to be estimated takes the form

$$\lambda(t,x) = \lambda_0(t)\exp(x_i\beta_i). \tag{3}$$

---

[88] With this approach I follow (Hendricks & Sorensen 2006; Hendricks & Sorensen 2009) who examine the time that music artists take between releases of albums. In order to be able to employ their implementation of a treatment effects model in the main analysis of their paper, the authors use a Cox model to test the critical assumption that the treatment is, after controlling for some determinants, random across artists. The methodological background will be described in more detail in chapter 5.3.2 which also builds on the authors' approach.

In the following section, I specify the set of variables that are included in the different specifications and estimation models.

Estimation models

The elapsed time between launches is computed as the number of weeks that an application was launched after the previous application in the portfolio: i.e., the lag of the second application to the first, the third application to the second, etc. These lags can be included in estimation models in two different ways. First, each lag, e.g. the time elapsed between application one and two in the portfolio, is estimated separately. Second, all lags are estimated simultaneously but controlled for by indicator variables. In the following, the main specification is reported separately for the second, third and fourth application as well as all lags jointly. The estimation models contain the determinants discussed in chapter 3.5.3.

3.5.4.3 Results

The results of the multivariate estimation are reported in Table 10. It contains the results that are based on a specification that is identical in terms of included regressors but differs in terms of applications included in the estimation. Columns (1) through (3) contain the results of separate estimations of the elapsed time between the launch of 452 second applications, 183 third applications and 99 fourth applications each after their previous application. The results in column (4) are the effects for all 906 applications estimated in one model but separated by indicator variables. All results are reported in form of Cox Hazard ratios. In the following, I present the results of column (4) and discuss if there are differences or trends that occur with regard to the entry order of applications.

Table 10: Results of Cox Model on time elapsed between application launches

VARIABLES	(1) elapsed time between 1 and 2	(2) elapsed time between 2 and 3	(3) elapsed time between 3 and 4	(4) elapsed time overall
Previous application characteristics				
first 4 weeks accum. usage of prev. app (in 100k)	1.070	1.010	0.886	0.967
	(0.0456)	(0.387)	(0.115)	(0.0226)
growth rate prev. app (in percent)	1.000	1.000**	1.000	1.000**
	(0.000035)	(0.000078)	(0.000288)	(0.000021)
num. of updates in prev. 2 weeks of prev. app	1.520***	2.099***	1.649***	1.604***
	(0.0549)	(0.114)	(0.116)	(0.0411)
num. of updates in prev. weeks 2 to 4 of prev. app	1.168***	1.418***	1.264***	1.208***
	(0.0281)	(0.0550)	(0.0765)	(0.0246)
Developer characteristics				
company dev (0/1)	0.891	1.268*	0.880	0.978
	(0.0799)	(0.182)	(0.155)	(0.0662)
dev experience at app launch (in weeks)	0.875***	0.922***	1.011	0.931***
	(0.0181)	(0.0178)	(0.0277)	(0.00884)
dev entry before Sept 02, 2007 (0/1)	2.880***	2.271***	0.638	1.611***
	(0.666)	(0.520)	(0.264)	(0.204)
num. installs by dev in week 34, 2007 (in million)	1.168**	1.177	1.160	1.072*
	(0.0739)	(0.178)	(0.164)	(0.0442)
Application characteristics				
app in same category as prev. app (0/1)	1.166**	0.950	1.694***	1.020
	(0.0899)	(0.131)	(0.322)	(0.0598)
entry order of app in dev portfolio (full sample)	1.017**	0.998	0.995	0.996***
	(0.00760)	(0.00327)	(0.00578)	(0.00137)
Market characteristics				
weeks since platform launch	1.085**	1.081	1.131	1.064**
	(0.0429)	(0.0625)	(0.133)	(0.0297)
number of apps in launch week (in '00s)	0.867***	0.867*	0.786	0.885***
	(0.0453)	(0.0650)	(0.126)	(0.0321)
HHI in app launch week	0.998***	0.996***	0.997	0.998***
	(0.000548)	(0.000959)	(0.00287)	(0.000409)
Observations	452	183	99	906
Chi2	503.7	414.8	229.1	966.9
Log-likelihood	-2157	-704.2	-344.9	-5029

Note: Reporting Cox Hazard Ratios. Category dummies included but not displayed. (4) includes but does not display entry order dummies. Rob. standard errors in parentheses. Sign. levels: *** p<0.01, ** p<0.05, * p<0.1.

It is an important finding that there appears to be no significant relationship between the usage pattern of the previous application and the time elapsed until the launch of the following application. Neither the success (measured by the first four weeks of accumulated usage of the previous application) nor the growth rate of the previous application have a consistently significant effect on the timing of the following application. Another characteristic of the previous application, however, has a significant effect. An additional update to the previous application in the two weeks prior to the launch of the following application (sample average is 1.84 updates (median: 0.00)) increases the probability of an application launch by about 60%. The increase is about 20% for an additional update in the four weeks prior to the launch. This indicates that the relationship between the effort spent on the most recent application and the time it takes to develop and launch the next application is not substitutive but rather facilitating: developers who are more active in the management of their existing applications release the next application sooner. The effect is consistent if one considers each of the application pairs separately (see columns (1) – (3)). The effect is strongest for the time elapsed between the second and third application. Thus, no clearly identifiable trend can be observed regarding the increasing age of the portfolio.

With respect to the developer characteristics, the estimation results reveal that developers with more experience at the time of the new application's launch take more time to develop and release the following application. Overall, an additional week of experience decreases the probability of launch by around 7%; see column (4)). This finding suggests that more experience does not necessarily lead to more or faster development and launch of applications. Rather, developers seem to release their applications early on in their interaction with Facebook's application platform. Interestingly, the effect is stronger for earlier applications in the portfolio (more than 12% for the time between application 1 and 2; see column (1)), decreases with every release and is insignificant for the time between applications 3 and 4 (see column (3)). On the other hand, there is a strong positive and significant effect of developer entry before September 2007 on the elapsed time between application releases. The probability of the launch of the second application is more than 180% higher for developers active before September 2007 (see column (1)). The effect decreases and is at around 120% for the time between application 2 and 3.[89] This finding is surprising. One would expect that developers that had been active for a longer time would release applications less frequently. An explanation for the finding would be if developers that were active before September 2007 are generally releasing more applications and, as a consequence, also more frequently. Finally, the estimated effects of the other determinants (whether the developer is a company or the number of installations before September 2007) are not, or not consistently across the three different transitions, significant.

The estimation results for effect of application characteristics on the time elapsed between application launches is mixed.[90] The probability of a launch is by about 16% higher for an application that is released within the same category as the previous application as opposed to an application that was released within a different category (see column (1)). The effect is even stronger, about 69%, for the time that elapses between application 3 and 4 (column (3)). However, the estimation results are insignificant for the time between application 2 and 3 (column (2)) as well as in the joint estimation of all applications (column (4)). Nevertheless, the results hint that release times are notably shorter between applications of the same category. This may indicate that applications are considered to be complements rather substitutes, especially within the portfolio of a developer. While it is unlikely that the complementarities are of functional nature, they may be based on certain spillover effects in the user activity (usage) of the applications. This question is examined in detail in chapter 5.

The results provide interesting insights in the impact of the market environment on the timing of application releases. First, the results indicate that time between application launches decreases as Facebook's platform for applications matures (as measured by weeks since platform launch in May 2007): an additional week increases the probability of an application launch by about 6% (see column (4)). The strength of the effect is consistent across the alternative specifications, however not significant for the time between the launch of applications 3 and 4. Another interesting finding relates to com-

---

[89] It is important to note that for developers that entered before September 2007, the applications in the sample are not the first applications overall but rather the first applications launched after September 2, 2007 by each developer (see section 2.4).

[90] The estimation results of the determinant that was included in the estimation in order to control for out-of-sample effects based on the overall entry order of the application (see section 3.5.3) are significant and report a minimal negative effect for the specification that estimates all applications jointly. The effect is significant and minimally positive for the time between application 1 and 2 but insignificant for the other applications. As a consequence, I conclude that the results are not sufficiently consistent to be interpreted.

petition on the platform. Overall, an increase in competition appears to prolong the time elapsed between application launches. For example, an additional 100 applications on the platform in the application's launch week decreases the probability of an application launch by about 12% (see column (4)). This effect is consistent and significant across the separate estimations.[91] Another measure for competition is the Herfindahl-Hirsch-Index (HHI): an increase in market concentration (as measured by the HHI) decreases the probability of launch for the following application. Thus, the results confirm the findings from the other measure, i.e. the number of applications on the platform. This finding is noteworthy as it separates the effect of competition from other applications from an overall time trend that captures the maturation of the platform. While the overall trend increases the probability of the next application's launch, the effect from competition decreases it. The differences in market environment are examined in more detail in an extension that utilizes the policy change to the platform for applications.[92]

The previously employed specification (as introduced in section 3.5.4.2) is modified and extended to estimate the influence that the policy change regarding notifications has on the elapsed time between application launches. In order to capture this effect, different approaches are taken. First, an indicator variable marking whether the new application is launched before or after the policy change is added. Secondly, the first specification is estimated separately for applications that launched before the policy change (denoted by "pre-PC" in the results table) or after the policy change ("post-PC"). The results of this modified specification are provided in Table 11.

---

[91] The result is insignificant but with consistent effect strength for the time between application 3 and 4 (see column (3)).

[92] See section 0 for a description and preliminary analysis of the policy change.

Table 11: Results of Cox Model (incl. policy change (i.e. PC))

VARIABLES	(1)	(2)	(3)	(4)
	time	*time*	*time*	*time*
	all apps - without PC	all apps - including PC	apps launched before PC	apps launched after PC
Previous application characteristics				
first 4 weeks accum. usage of prev. app (in 100k)	0.967	0.969	0.967	1.054
	(0.0226)	(0.0228)	(0.0248)	(0.0641)
growth rate prev. app (in percent)	1.000**	1.000	1.000	1.000
	(0.000021)	(0.000022)	(0.000052)	(0.000027)
num. of updates in prev. 2 weeks of prev. app	1.604***	1.619***	1.610***	1.788***
	(0.0411)	(0.0400)	(0.0451)	(0.0991)
num. of updates in prev. weeks 2 to 4 of prev. app	1.208***	1.223***	1.224***	1.218***
	(0.0246)	(0.0217)	(0.0233)	(0.0568)
Developer characteristics				
company dev (0/1)	0.978	0.995	1.013	0.811
	(0.0662)	(0.0656)	(0.0719)	(0.157)
dev experience at app launch (in weeks)	0.931***	0.931***	0.913***	0.943***
	(0.00884)	(0.00871)	(0.0110)	(0.0179)
dev entry before Sept 02, 2007 (0/1)	1.611***	1.610***	1.778***	2.979**
	(0.204)	(0.204)	(0.271)	(1.379)
num. installs by dev in week 34, 2007 (in million)	1.072*	1.082*	1.118***	0.851
	(0.0442)	(0.0442)	(0.0460)	(0.565)
Application characteristics				
app in same category as prev. app (0/1)	1.020	1.027	1.017	1.480**
	(0.0598)	(0.0588)	(0.0609)	(0.273)
entry order of app in dev portfolio (full sample)	0.996***	0.996***	0.995***	1.006
	(0.00137)	(0.00136)	(0.00155)	(0.00984)
Market characteristics				
weeks since platform launch	1.064**	1.021	1.036	0.383*
	(0.0297)	(0.0390)	(0.0392)	(0.211)
app launch after notification change in 2008w7 (0/1)		3,621***		
		(10,372)		
number of apps in launch week (in '00s)	0.885***	0.929	0.918*	2.461
	(0.0321)	(0.0419)	(0.0416)	(1.513)
policy change interaction: num. apps (in '00s)		0.941		
		(0.0467)		
HHI in app launch week	0.998***	0.999***	0.999***	0.969***
	(0.000409)	(0.000417)	(0.000435)	(0.0117)
policy change interaction: HHI		0.970**		
		(0.0123)		
Observations	906	906	748	158
Chi2	966.9	1030	907.1	404.7
Log-likelihood	-5029	-5024	-4001	-591.7

Note: Reporting Cox Hazard Ratios. Category dummies and entry order dummies included but not displayed. Rob. standard errors in parentheses. Sign. levels: *** p<0.01, ** p<0.05, * p<0.1.

The estimation results (see column (2) in Table 11, i.e. all 906 applications including the indicator variable for an entry before or after the policy change) are largely unchanged to the results presented above.[93] This provides a welcome robustness check and increases the confidence in the results. However, and expectedly, there are differences in the effects relating to the market characteristics at application launch. The indicator variable that separates applications launched before and after the policy change is highly significant and strongly positive. Including the indicator (and its interactions with the measures of application competition) changes the results from the previous specification. The effects for the overall time trend of the maturing platform as well as the number of applications as measure for competition are not significant in the specification including the indicator. The effect for market concentration based on the Herfindahl-Hirsch-Index remains unchanged. In this specification the strength of the effect of the indicator variable is startling. The hazard ratio of 3,621 is unusually high and cannot be explained. As a consequence, one needs to be cautions in interpreting the results (even though the consistency with the previous results is re-confirming).

In order to examine this result further, the original specification is estimated separately for the applications launched before and after the policy change. Again, the results for the previous application and developer characteristics are qualitatively and quantitatively unchanged. There are, however, differences in the application-specific characteristics. Regarding the launch of the application within the same category as the previous application, the estimation results are insignificant for the group of applications launched before the policy change (thus, in line with the overall estimation). The effect is positive and significant for applications launched after the policy change. Here, applications launched in the same category have a 48% higher probability to be launched in the next period. This finding suggests that developers specialize as the platform matures and aim at providing multiple applications in the same category in order to maintain a high level of activity of their existing user base.[94]

Finally, there are differences between the two groups of applications with regard to the influence of market characteristics on the elapsed time between application launches. The effect of the overall time trend measuring the maturation of the platform is insig-

---

[93] See column (1) in Table 11 which is identical to column (4) of Table 10.

[94] The effect of the overall entry order is consistent with the previous findings for the group of applications launched before the policy change and insignificant for the group launched after the change.

nificant (even though consistent with the prior reported results) for applications launched before the policy change. Interestingly, the effect changes, however, for applications launched after the change. Here, the probability of a launch of the following application decreases by around 62% for every additional week.[95] This finding differs from the results of the estimation that includes all applications and which reports an effect that increases the probability by around 6%. Since this time trend potentially captures many different effects,[96] it is interesting to examine whether the measures for market concentration and competition explain this change. The results, however, are inconclusive. On the one hand, the prolonging effect on the time elapsed from an increase in the market concentration (i.e. measured by the Herfindahl-Hirsch-Index) is higher for the group of applications launched after the policy change (compare the hazard ratio of 0.969 vs. 0.999). On the other hand, the effect from the number of applications on the platform is not significant for this group (it is significant and consistent with the previous results for the group of applications launched before the policy change). The findings, as a consequence, only hint an explanation for the change.

The following section concludes this analysis by summarizing and discussing the findings.

3.5.5 Conclusion

After the previous analysis of the overall platform, the aggregate statistics of applications as well as the policy change, this section focused on the portfolios of applications by developers. Apart from anecdotal observations in popular publications, there exists neither a conceptual nor an empirical analysis of a representative sample of developer portfolios on the Facebook platform. As a consequence, this section aimed at providing additional insights into secondary interdependencies in developer portfolios. The findings contribute to a better understanding of the context of the subsequent analysis of usage interdependencies (spillovers) between applications (see chapter 5).

A first analysis examined differences between single-app and portfolio developers. The main finding is that the vast majority of developers only have one application in

---

[95] The effect is significant at the 10% level.
[96] The time trend captures the effect of the maturing platform within each group of applications. This means that it only differs within the group of applications launched before and after the policy change.

their portfolio.[97] Furthermore, if a developer manages a portfolio, it is likely to be small. Only 83 developers (around 18% of portfolio developers) have three applications and 39 developers (around 9%) manage four applications. These results are surprising, because it is assumed that the cost of developing an application is very low (particularly when considering the learning effects after having built the first application). Another finding is that portfolio developers seem to be more successful in the sample period. This preliminary analysis, however, does not allow drawing causal conclusions concerning the dynamics and incentives of developers to build application portfolios. In order to address this caveat, additional studies both with theoretical and empirical emphasis need to be conducted.

A second analysis examined the determinants that influence the time that elapses between application launches of portfolio developers, a secondary interdependence between applications that is of interest for the subsequent analysis in chapter 5. Despite its multivariate setup, it also is of exploratory nature. The estimation identifies several significant effects. For example, an increase in the update frequency of the previous application's directory page leads to a shorter time between application launches. An increase in competition, as measured by number of applications and the Herfindahl-Hirsch-Index, on the other hand prolongs the time between releases. Interestingly, there is no significant effect of the previous application's usage pattern on the elapsed time. This is surprising because one would assume that the success and the growth or decline path of a developer's existing applications has an influence on the developer's incentives and strategic decision making of whether and when to launch another application. An explanation for the lack of significant empirical evidence could be that the usage of application is highly skewed across applications and rather volatile within each application.

The empirical analyses of this section provide a first glimpse into the composition of developer portfolios as well as their management. Additional research, should investigate what determines the decision of developers to launch more than one application as well as the sequence and the timing in more detail. This requires both additional work on the theoretical foundation of these questions as well as more empirical studies, possibly involving additional data gathering on both the developer and application level. For the purpose of providing the background for the following chapters of this

---

[97] Note that the sample selection criteria of section 3.2 apply.

dissertation, the exploratory character of this section was valuable. Given the lack of previous work in the field, both theoretical and empirical, this section in fact offers some contribution to the emerging field of an applied analysis of software platforms and application eco-systems.

3.6 Chapter summary

This chapter builds on the more general description of Facebook and its platform (see section 1.4.2) and focuses on the developers and their applications. Its main purpose was to provide the reader with detailed background knowledge on the empirical context and the data set of this dissertation. I analyzed and described different aspects of both the empirical context and other, secondary interdependencies that exist on Facebook's platform for applications.

After a detailed description of the sampling process (see section 3.2), it presented several empirical analyses that examine the platform, developers and applications from various perspectives. Due to the lack of previous, both theoretical and empirical, work in the field, the character of these analyses was predominantly exploratory. Nevertheless, they led to several interesting findings (which are summarized and discussed in the respective sections) that contribute to the emerging body of work on internet-based software platforms and application eco-systems (Evans et al. 2006; Boudreau 2008a; Boudreau & Hagiu 2010).

Another important contribution of this chapter is the in-depth analysis and verification of the original data set and the sampling decisions made. In the course of conducting the various analyses, results were computed for the sample (as described in section 3.2) and for the full data set.[98] This approach further confirmed the choice of sampling criteria and strengthens the confidence in the representativeness and adequacy of the sample.[99] An illustration for this finding is that, even though the portfolio size is directly influenced by the minimum criteria of application usage, the number of applications by each developer is similarly distributed in both the sample and the full data set.

---

[98] The results of this and the following chapters are based on the sampled data. Documentation and log-files of the results based on the full data set are available from the author upon request.

[99] Note that this sample is based on the available data after crawling and parsing the directory. An additional, potential bias remains if applications or developers were not included in this original data set (see chapter 2).

4   Interdependencies between users

4.1   Chapter overview

The adoption and diffusion patterns of new products have long been of interest to scholars from management and economics. A plethora of studies aimed at explaining the emergence of the typical S-shaped diffusion curve (Rogers 1983) and identified various drivers that influence the diffusion and adoption of new products. In the management literature (predominantly stemming from marketing, new product development and innovation research) it is widely accepted that product adoption and diffusion is influenced by an individual's (i.e. potential adopter's) social environment (Hill et al. 2006; Van den Bulte & Stremersch 2004; Aral & Walker 2010). In this literature, an actor's adoption decision is seen as a function of his information on other actors' knowledge, attitudes and behavior regarding a novel product. Here, it has been shown that product adoption can be driven by social influence that is often based on word of mouth (WOM) recommendations of other actors and that adoption spreads from actor to actor.[100] Economists, on the other hand, emphasize the importance of network externalities as important drivers of diffusion and product adoption: The utility derived from the adoption of products exhibiting network externalities increases in the size of the installed base of users. Hence, adoption probabilities for potential adopters are increasing in the size of the existing network (Katz & Shapiro 1985). Social influence as well as existence of network externalities can lead to positive interdependencies accelerating the diffusion of new products significantly once a critical mass of consumers have been reached (Tirole 1988; Valente 1996).

Against the backdrop of a growing importance of products based on digital technologies that facilitate information exchange between different actors, there has been an increasing interest in a refined understanding of mechanisms that create positive interdependencies between users. In fact, companies' marketing strategies are more frequently focusing on the active management of WOM communication and viral spread of information via IT-based communication channels to achieve accelerated product adoption (Mayzlin 2006; Godes & Mayzlin 2009). Examples include internet-based services that allow users to "invite" their friends to join the service via referral mes-

---

[100] Information that spreads from actor to actor is also called "viral" (Subramani & Rajagopalan 2003; Aral & Walker 2010).

sages such as email providers (e.g., Google's Gmail) or Facebook with its online social network and application platform.

Consequently, recent research turned to the question which characteristics make products more "viral" than others (Stephen & Berger 2009), what type of WOM fosters product sales (Godes & Mayzlin 2009) and the relation of network effects on product choice (Corrocher & Zirulia 2009). Most recently and – perhaps most importantly - Aral & Walker (2010) analyze how product design can foster viral spread and positive interdependencies in the spread of an application within Facebook's application platform. In a randomized experiment they find that the inclusion of viral features (the two primary features are notifications and personal referrals or invitations) in a product can greatly increase adoption by actors that experience either passive-broadband or active-personalized influence by their peers.

This chapter builds on this literature and contains an empirical study of the discovery and adoption of Facebook applications.[101] The focus is on interdependencies between users in those decisions. The chapter contributes to the research on social influence and network externalities (as reviewed in section 1.3.2) in two ways.

First, unlike previous studies, it aims at analyzing the effect of social influence and network externalities on product adoption simultaneously. Existing studies predominantly focus either on the effect of social influence (Van den Bulte & Stremersch 2004; Aral & Walker 2010) or the effect of network externalities on product adoption (Katz & Shapiro 1985; Corrocher & Zirulia 2009). The choice of a more comprehensive framework encompassing both social influence as well as network effects allows drawing a more refined picture of the user-interdependent mechanisms that lead to positive interdependencies or "viral" spread of adoption.

Second, and equally important, the study is not confined to the analysis of product adoption. It also examines the circumstances in which actors who already adopted a new product choose to promote an application by actively exerting influence to stimulate adoption amongst their peers. As the circle of contagion is closed by the recommendations of adopters, examining the drivers behind active recommendations is central to understanding the implications for optimal product configurations. In this context, Subramani & Rajagopalan (2003) pointed to the fact that adopters' inclination to

---

[101] The chapter is based on joint-research project with Rebecca Ermecke and Stefan Wagner. An earlier version of section 4.4 was published in Ermecke et al. (2009).

pass on information to their peers might be a function of existing network externalities. This study takes on this argument and following Henkel & Block (2008) distinguishes the effect of local and global network externalities on adopters' recommendation behavior.

In contrast to related studies that make use of crawler-data such as Aral et al. (2009) or Aral & Walker (2010), this study is based on survey data on individual adoption and recommendation decisions. The data was collected via an internet-based questionnaire among users of the popular online network Facebook in February 2008. 358 respondents indicated their reasons for choosing to adopt and to promote applications, which are add-on services to Facebook and enrich the user experience.

The setting is suitable for a study of adoption and social influence for two reasons. First, on Facebook, applications are developed and marketed by external developers and offered free-of charge. This allows me to isolate the influence of product characteristics and social interaction without having to control for heterogeneity in the willingness-to-pay of potential adopters.[102] Second, the Facebook service provides channels for the transmission of information that allow analyzing the effect of social influence in both active and passive forms and, thus, similar to Aral & Walker (2010).

This chapter is organized as follows: I begin with a conceptual framework that introduces the adoption and promotion decisions and describes the relationships and hypotheses I am most interested in. In section 4.3, I introduce the research design by describing the empirical setting and the data source. Next, in section 4.4, I present findings of a descriptive analysis of the data. A multivariate analysis and its findings are presented in section 0. The chapter concludes with a summary, implications and suggestions for further research.

4.2   Conceptual model and hypotheses

This study examines different effects that social influence and network effects exert on the decisions of individuals to adopt and to promote a new product. For this purpose, the study proposes a conceptual model with product adoption as a first decision and product promotion (i.e. active influence to use a product) as a second decision. The

---

[102] Note that users will have different willingness to spend time on learning about and using a new application. This form of heterogeneity needs to be controlled for in the following analysis.

model takes into account that social influence and network effects are primary determinants of individuals' choices on both stages. Figure 13 contains a graphical representation of the conceptual model. The left part refers to individuals who are potential adopters of the product confronted with the decision to adopt or not. This decision might depend - amongst others– on the active or passive influence exerted by their peers as well as perceived benefit from network externalities. The right part of Figure 13 relates to individuals who are already users of an innovative product or service. Users of a product can choose to promote this product to their peers and hence to exert active influence on others. This decision is analyzed in a second step. In the following, I present a detailed explanation of the model components.

Figure 13: Decisions in network markets in the presence of social influence.

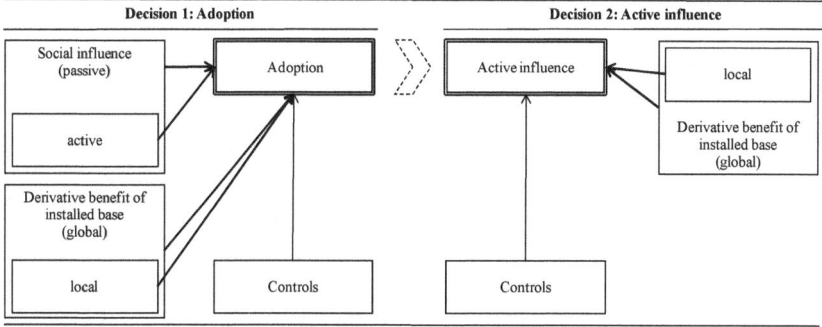

Decision 1: Adoption

To summarize, product adoption in the model is a function of social influence, the perception of network externalities as well as additional determinants, which are represented by the "controls" box.

Social influence

Following the literature review in 1.3.2, social influence is distinguished in terms of the role of the influencing individual. The study first examines how *passive social influence* affects the adoption decision of new products. This is the case if existing users of a product do not intend to influence potential adopters but rather unintentionally send signals about different characteristics, e.g. quality or simply usage of the service. These signals are received by potential adopters and, following the notion of normative (i.e. conformity) and informational (i.e. reduction of complexity) social influence, lead to an increased probability of adoption (Deutsch & Gerard 1955; Banerjee 1992; Bikhchandani et al. 1998). Hence, my first hypothesis is:

> *H1-1a: Potential users are more likely to adopt a service, the more passive influence they are exposed to.*

Second, social influence can take the form of a user's purposeful action and an intended recommendation to their peers. I will refer to this form of social influence as *active social influence*. One stream of literature refers to active social influence (recommendations) as word-of-mouth communication, which is regarded as "informal, person-to-person communication between a perceived non-commercial communicator and a receiver regarding a brand, a product, an organization, or a service" (Harrison-Walker 2001). Exposure to favorable word-of-mouth was found to increase the probability of purchase, whereas exposure to unfavorable comments decreased the probability (Arndt 1967). In accordance with this prior evidence, the first hypothesis H1 is:

> *H1-1b: Potential users are more likely to adopt a service, the more active influence they are exposed to.*

Perception of network effects

From the perspective of an individual, the utility of using a product that exhibits network effects, by definition, increases in the number of total users (installed-base). The decision to adopt a product with network effects, therefore, is a function of the size of its installed based and the expectations on the future growth of this installed base (Katz & Shapiro 1985). Network effects can be differentiated into global and local network effects (Koski & Kretschmer 2004). Network effects are global when the utility of an individual from using a good is influenced by the total number of other users. Network effects are said to be local when the utility is influenced by particular individuals only. While most of the literature focuses on global network externalities, there are cases where a user is less interested in the anonymous mass of other users but rather in a relevant subset thereof (e.g. users within specific geographical boundaries, personal contacts or people who share the same interests). For the following analysis, local network effects will be defined in terms of personal networks. Network effects are captured by the following two hypotheses:

H1-2a: Users are more likely to adopt a service, the higher they perceive the local network effects to be.

H1-2b: Users are more likely to adopt a service, the higher they perceive the global network effects to be.

Based on the argument above, it is also assumed that the perception of local externalities has a stronger effect than the perception of global network effects:

H1-2c: The effect of a potential adopter's perception of local network effects on his probability to adopt a product is stronger than the effect of his perception of global network effects.

Further Determinants of Product Adoption

This paper develops a conceptual model that extends the previous literature and focuses specifically on the distinction between different forms of social influence and the perception of network effects. However, one must not neglect additional determinants that influence the utility assessment of a novel service and, thus, the adoption decision. In empirical analyses, these need to be controlled for. For one, there are considerations of economic utility, namely the costs of acquiring and using a service as well as the benefit that usage entails. The theory on diffusion of innovations and the adoption decision of individuals (Rogers 1983) lends additional determinants, particularly concerning the characteristics of the innovation itself: ease of use or sources of risk, uncertainty or general opportunity costs of adoption. Also, characteristics of the prospective adopter are of importance. The adoption decision may, for example, be influenced by a user's general propensity to adopt products at a certain phase of its lifecycle. Individuals who tend to adopt early are known as innovators and early adopters. They may also exhibit characteristics of lead users (Von Hippel 1988). Finally, demographics, such as the age of the adopter or his nationality (due to cultural differences), may play a role.

Decision 2: Active influence

The second decision in a model of social influence in network markets relates to a user's decision of whether or not to actively influence others. Again, this decision depends on the individual's utility function. The focus of the study is on effects that constitute the interdependence between users in their decision to adopt, use and recommend applications. Consequently I am most interested in the effect that originates from a user's perception of the service's network effects. The expected influence of this effect as well as additional determinants are discussed in the following.

Perception of network effects

Recent theoretical work by Henkel & Block (2008) studies the relationship between an early adopter's incentive to influence peers and their perception of network effects. Since existing users benefit from additional users joining as users of the service, they are willing to incur costs of "sponsoring" new users. They are willing to alleviate the disutility incurred by new adopters by investing time and effort to explain the product, to offer consulting or to reduce search costs. This positive feedback mechanism of network externalities was first introduced by Block & Koellinger (2007) and labeled "peer effect". The authors define it as an active and purposeful action via normative influence by a user, who is motivated by the incentive to increase his utility through altering his interaction possibilities. They also present first empirical evidence. For a survey among users of two internet services, the authors find significant evidence that the peer-effect explains adoption of the service with network effects (instant messaging), while such an effect could not be found for a good without network effects (online banking). Since sponsoring becomes a public good and is, thus, prone to shirking and free riding, the peer effect is strongest in small networks (Henkel & Block 2008). This is consistent with theory on local versus global network effects. Based on this recent work, I formulate the hypotheses:

H2-1: Users are more likely to exert active influence, the stronger they perceive network effects to be.

H2-1a: An increase in the perception of local network effects increases the propensity to exert active influence more than an increase in the perception of global network effects.

Additional determinants (Controls)

There exist additional factors that determine the choice to exert active influence. These factors need to be considered as controls in an empirical model. Such additional determinants should include the cost of exerting influence and costs of contacting one's peers as well as a series of other factors such as an assessment of the service as well as characteristics of the active user. Examples for the latter are opinion leadership (Katz & Lazarsfeld 1955) and demographics such age, nationality and gender. For example, Feick & Price (1987) find for a sample of U.S. consumers that recommending individuals are more likely to be female. Wiedmann et al. (2001) find the same for a sample of German consumers.

4.3 Research design

In contrast to related studies on Facebook that make use of crawler-data such as Aral et al. (2009) or Aral & Walker (2010), this study is based on survey data on individual adoption and recommendation decisions. The data was collected via an internet-based questionnaire targeted at Facebook users in February 2008. At that time, Facebook accounted for more than 50 million active users worldwide and there were more than 15,000 applications on the platform. More than 90% of Facebook's users had installed and used at least one application.[103]

This setting is suitable for two reasons. First, Facebook provides a technical infrastructure that allows external developers to write software applications which expand the platform's functionality. Applications can be added to and removed from profiles at the user's discretion and their vast majority is entirely free of charge.[104] Installation of applications is easy as users can browse and install applications within Facebook without the necessity to visit the manufacturers homepage for a download or to install software on their desktop computer. This setting offers a unique opportunity to study the determinants of product adoption relevant to the study: as the price[105] or the availability of the products in question is not a limiting factor for adoption, this setting al-

---

[103] See section 1.4.2 for a more detailed description of the Facebook service.
[104] Only very few applications have a premium version that gives users additional functionality for a small fee.
[105] An individual does incur costs in form of time commitment for using a new application. Here, preferences are likely to be heterogeneous. This needs to be controlled for in the following analysis.

lows me to focus on the impact of social influence on the adoption decision and on product characteristics such as network externalities induced by the use of certain applications.

The second reason is that Facebook's interface provides clear channels for the transmission of information that allows me to analyze the effect of social influence – both in its passive and active forms – on adoption decisions in a precise way. A prominent feature of Facebook's interface is the News Feed which contains updates on changes to profiles a user has linked to his own profile (Günther et al. 2010; Naaman et al. 2010). For example, any time a user adopts an application other users that linked his profile are notified of this activity as it appears on the News Feed on their own profile page.[106] This constitutes a form of passive social influence. At the same time, Facebook's functionality also allows its users to actively contact, recommend or point each other to new applications without much effort (a mouse click). With these "personalized referrals" (Aral & Walker 2010), users can choose to actively pass on information on certain applications and thus exert active social influence.

The questionnaire design and data collection were conducted in two steps. In a first exploratory step, interviews were conducted with both application users and developers.[107] In addition to insights that could be gained on Facebook-specific conferences, three semi-structured interviews with developers of popular applications provided insights into the design of applications. The objective of the developer interviews was to enquire of what the developers thought would help their applications to spread among the social network and the design tricks they used to encourage adoption. Moreover, five semi-structured interviews were conducted with Facebook users which helped to get additional insights into their general Facebook usage behavior. The more important objective of these user interviews was to get detailed information on the decision-making process preceding the installation of applications as well as the decision to actively recommend applications to friends.

In a second step, an online survey of Facebook users was conducted. The questionnaire was based on the insights from the exploratory interviews as well as on an in-depth literature review. It was developed in December 2007 and pretested in various

---

[106] Aral & Walker (2010) call this mechanism "automated broadcast information".

[107] The interviews and the additional information on Facebook Platform were gathered from US developers and sources. In the early phase of the platform, most developers and the main players in the ecosystem were located in the United States.

stages. The pretesting involved both paper-based questionnaires as well as an electronic version of the survey. In the final questionnaire, respondents were confronted with a choice of nine applications and were requested to pick one application they had heard of. For the remainder of the questionnaire, respondents were asked to answer a series of questions related to their adoption decision, whether they had actively passed on information on that application to other users and also their experience with that particular application. Moreover, all respondents answered a base set of questions concerning their personality, their general usage of Facebook as well as socio-demographic attributes such as age, gender and nationality.

internet-based survey designs are prone to a number of potential biases (Roztocki 2001). In particular, a non-response bias might exist if some users (e.g. due to their general interest in the field) find it more interesting to participate in the survey than others (Armstrong & Overton 1977). In this setting, it was tested whether users that adopted an application or users that decided to actively influence others were more or less likely to participate than users that did not. To test for this potential bias, the frequency of adopters and influencers among the earliest and the last ten percent of respondents were compared. A simple test for differences of means did not show a higher frequency of adopters/influencers answering early on – this suggests that there is no response bias in this respect.

Due to the strict policies of Facebook with regard to identifying and contacting its users, it was not possible to draw a random sample from the population of Facebook users. Instead, invitations to the survey had to be distributed through a very broad selection of different channels. The link to the survey was posted on more than 40 Facebook user groups as well as on a variety of online discussion boards, blogs, college websites, forums and mailing lists in various countries and institutions. This ensured that various groups of users would become aware of the survey.

4.4 Descriptive analysis

The adoption of third-party applications on Facebook can occur in three different settings: A user might become aware of a specific application independently of other users and install it. Awareness and adoption might also be triggered by observing other users' adoption decisions (in particular via the News Feed or by browsing other people's profile pages). Finally, users could also be made aware of applications by recommendations they receive from other users.

The following descriptive statistics present first findings from the survey which shed some light on the relative importance of the three alternatives. Moreover, it investigates whether there are differences in the probability that an application is finally adopted by a user depending on the way he was made aware of it. Finally, it also presents evidence on characteristics and motivations of users who actively pass on information to their peers.

4.4.1 How do users get aware of available applications?

Participants in the survey were confronted with nine applications and were asked to choose one application they had heard of. They were then asked how they first found out about this application. Viral channels (observation of users' behavior in the News Feed or receiving recommendations) played an overwhelming role compared to self-discovery by e.g. browsing the directory of applications or noticing the application in advertisements. At an aggregated level, viral channels account for far more than 90% of first contacts with an application (see Table 12).

Table 12: "How did you first take notice of the application?"

		N	%
	"I do not remember"	18	5.07
Passive viral channels	*"I observed that someone else was using it"*	149	44.79
Active viral channels	*"Someone invited me or told me about it"*	167	47.04
Non-viral channels	*"I found out about the application by myself"*	11	3.1
	Total	**355**	**100**

In a subsequent question, the participants that had not indicated not remembering their first contact were asked to provide further details about the way they became aware of the application. With regard to passive social channels (observation of others), about 30% of the respondents discovered the application on other's profile pages while only 10% mentioned the News Feed. Within the category of active viral channels, the most frequent response was the receipt of an invitation to install the application (about 38%). Only 12% of the respondents were prompted by the application because someone had tried to interact with them via the application.[108] Other active communication channels seem to have played a less important role, adding up to not even 5% of the

---

[108] An interaction attempt refers to a message that is sent another user in order to alert him to perform a certain task in the context of the application.

answers (see Table 13). Likewise, non-viral channels played almost no role: less than 4% of respondents indicated to have discovered the application via advertisement, the Facebook directory or through reports on another web page on the internet (e.g. blogs).

Table 13: "Please specify how you found out about the application"[109]

		N	%
	Don't remember	4	1.2
Passive viral channels	*Profile page*	104	31.14
	News Feed	25	10.48
	Request	126	37.72
	Interaction attempt	39	11.68
Active viral channels	*Other FB channel*	6	1.80
	Other online channel	4	1.20
	Offline channels	5	1.50
	Directory	6	1.80
Non-viral channels	*Internet*	3	0.90
	Advertisement	2	0.60
	Total	**334**	**100**

This indicates that viral channels are the most important source of information about new applications. Passive and active social influences are almost equally important in drawing users' awareness to third-party applications. Observation of other people's profile pages turned out to be the most important passive viral channel while invitations sent by other users constitute the most important active channel.

4.4.2   What drives adoption of applications?

While respondents were first asked whether they had heard of a specific application, they were subsequently asked whether they had later added this application to their profile. In total, 168 respondents (about 47%) indicated they had done so for the application they chose in the survey. This suggests that active recommendations by other users are the most important determinant of the diffusion of new applications. This is particularly interesting when compared to the findings in the previous section. While active and passive channels are equally important in drawing users' attention to applications, active channels seem to induce subsequent installations more frequently.

---

[109] The full question was: "Please specify how you observed that someone else was using/ how you were told/ how you found out about the application".

Table 14 reports the frequencies of different reasons to install an application. Interestingly, active channels of social influence account for almost 60% of installations, while the observation of others in contrast plays a minor role. Only 24% of the respondents indicated that passive influence triggered their decision to add the application. Information that the participants found via other channels accounted for 9% of the installation decisions.

This suggests that active recommendations by other users are the most important determinant of the diffusion of new applications. This is particularly interesting when compared to the findings in the previous section. While active and passive channels are equally important in drawing users' attention to applications, active channels seem to induce subsequent installations more frequently.

Table 14: "What was the main trigger to add the application?"

	N	%	Cum.
Invited / interaction	98	59.04	59.04
Observed	40	24.10	83.13
Self-discovered	15	9.04	92.17
Don't remember	13	7.83	100.00
Total	**166**	**100**	

4.4.3 Who does actively recommend?

The findings of the previous section suggest that user recommendations are particularly effective in fostering the diffusion of applications. This section further examines the characteristics and motives of users who actively recommended applications. Only users who had installed an application themselves were asked about their invitation behavior.

Table 15: Active influencers by gender

	Active influencer	Non-influencer	Total
Female	71	37	**108**
Male	23	37	**60**
Total	**94**	**74**	**168**

Note: Pearson chi2(1) = 11.77 ; p-value = 0.001

Characteristics of active recommenders

About 56 % of the users who installed an application actively recommended it to at least one of their friends. Table 15 shows that female respondents in the sample were more likely to be active influencers than men (the test on the difference of means is highly significant).

Figure 14: Number of recommendations sent to peers (by gender)[110]

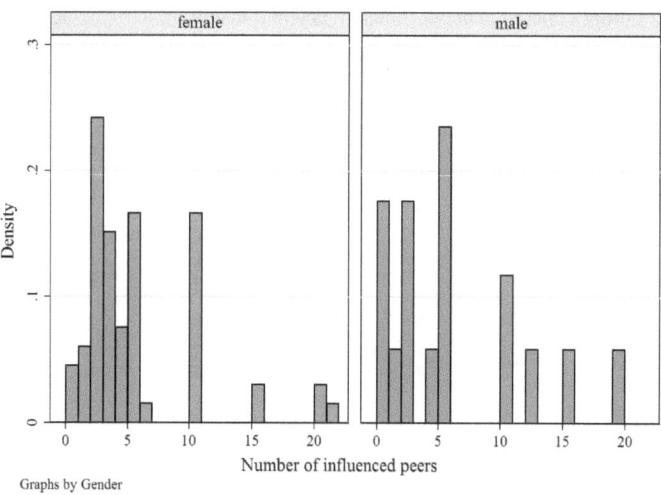

Graphs by Gender

On average, recommendations were sent to about 11.6 contacts (N = 89 of 168; s.d.: 42.62; min.: 0; median: 4.0; max.: 400). There are no clear gender differences with regard to the number of recommendations sent to peers (Figure 14 shows the distribution of recommendations separated by gender).[111] Users on average estimated the success rates of their invitations to be slightly over 60% (N = 79 of 168; s.d.: 0.33; min.: 0; median: 0.60; max.: 1.00).[112] Interestingly, social contagion through active channels

---

[110] This figure plots observations with up to 25 recommendations. Six observations with outlier values are excluded.

[111] A t-test on the difference of the means is insignificant when the outliers in the sample are excluded (see [110]).

[112] This conversion rate is computed as a fraction of the number of peers that respondents estimate to have installed the application (N = 85 of 168; mean: 4.98; s.d.: 11.47; min.: 0; median: 2.00; max.: 100) and the above mentioned number of recommendations sent to peers.

does not seem to work through few very active users but rather through a broad base of influencers – the median indicates that 50% of the respondents sent not more than 4 recommendations. While users issue targeted recommendations to a small number of friends, the impact of this behavior is shown by high reported conversion rates.

Furthermore, users that actively sent recommendations differ from users who have not sent recommendations with regard to their perception of the application at the time of installation (see Table 16). Users who had not recommended the application to their peers were more concerned about their privacy and installing to many applications that would clutter their profile page than users who recommended the application. No significant differences between the two groups of users can be found when looking at the ease of installations and the fear of wasting too much time.

Table 16: Perception of the application by influencing behavior

	Active influencer		Non-influencer		Diff.
	Mean	S.D.	Mean	S.D.	p-value
"Using the app seemed to be pretty easy and self-explanatory"	4.31	0.75	4.22	0.76	0.21
"I was afraid that my profile would appear messy if I added the app"	2.56	1.43	3.01	1.53	0.03
"I was afraid, that adding the app would endanger my privacy"	1.85	1.12	2.30	1.29	0.01
"I was afraid that using the app might make me waste time"	2.21	1.20	2.36	1.21	0.21

Note: N= 94 (active influencer), N = 74 (non-influencer); one-sided p-values for significantly smaller or larger means respectively.

Motivation to actively recommend

Different items related to motivational aspects proposed by previous studies (Henkel & Block 2008) were included in the questionnaire and presented to those respondents who had indicated to have sent recommendations to other people. Altruistic aspects received the highest agreement rates. For example, the statement "I thought other people would find the application useful or entertaining. Therefore, I told my friends about it." received strongest agreement, followed by the motive to share enthusiasm (see Table 17). On the other hand, more selfish motivations that referred to increasing one's own benefit via invitations earned lesser agreement. The particular low agreement to the item related to extrinsic rewards has implications for practitioners who seek to incentivize product recommendations. While adding features that bring about local network effects and further increase the benefit from getting friends to use the application as well could possibly increase recommendations, designing explicit reward schemes might not warrant the effort as they are not a strong motivation for making recommendations.

Table 17: "Please indicate your motivation to tell someone about the application"

	N	Mean	S.D.	Median
"I thought other people would find the app useful or entertaining".	91	4.18	0.88	4.0
"I just wanted to share enthusiasm or frustration that I experienced with the app"	88	3.25	1.25	4.0
"The app is more useful to me the more of my friends use the app"	88	3.09	1.29	3.5
"The app is more useful to me the more other people use the app"	88	2.39	1.29	2.0
"I could earn rewards within the app for recruiting friends"	88	1.92	1.33	1.0

Note: Answers on 5-point rating scale, min=1, max=5 for each item.

Communication channels of active recommendation

The enquiry which communication channels are used to pass on recommendations shows that the built-in recommendation functions are much more frequently used than alternative communication channels (such as other Facebook channels or other online or offline communication, see Table 18). Thus, designing mechanisms for easy invitations and reduced friction of recommendations seems to pay off by encouraging diffusion.

Table 18: "What channels did you use to tell about the application?"

	N	%
"I used the built-in feature to invite friends"	80	71.43
"I told someone offline about the application"	16	14.29
"I used other FB communication to tell friends"	10	8.93
"I told people using some sort of other online com."	6	5.36
Total	**112**	**100**

Note: Multiple answers were allowed to this question.

After this descriptive analysis, I now turn to the multivariate analysis of the two decisions described in the conceptual model.

4.5   Multivariate analysis

This section contains the multivariate analysis of the adoption and influence decisions that were discussed in section 4.2. It first defines the variables used in the analysis (section 4.5.1) and then introduces the empirical model used (section 4.5.2). The results are presented and discussed in section 4.5.3.

4.5.1   Variables

This section introduces and defines the measurement of the variables in each model.[113] I begin with the two dependent variables indicating the adoption and active influence decision. The independent variables denote the measures needed to test the hypotheses of section 4.2. The section closes with a description of the control variables.

4.5.1.1 Dependent variables

Model 1 – Adoption decision: The adoption of an application is simply measured by asking survey participants to indicate whether they have previously installed an application (added the application to their profile). This variable takes the values 0 or 1.

Model 2 – Active influence decision: Participants were asked whether they ever suggested another person to use an application. This variable takes the values 0 or 1.

4.5.1.2 Independent variables

I distinguish between the perception of social influence, with the two types of active and passive influence, and the perception of network effects.

Perception of social influence (Adoption model only)

There is no single definition of social influence and accordingly there is no established way to measure the extent to which social influence was exerted. Because of this lack of established measurements an operationalization was chosen that is easy to understand and, thus, does not put a burden on the participants of the survey. In particular, single-item measurements were used wherever possible.

---

[113] In addition to the detailed descriptive analysis in section 4.4, summary statistics of the variables are provided in the appendix to chapter 4.

(1) Experience of passive social influence: The key feature of passive social influence is that potential adopters become aware of the behavior of their peers by observing their choices and behavior. A simple measure whether passive social influence was experienced when deciding on the adoption of a certain application was constructed by asking respondents whether they were aware that at least one of their Facebook friends was using the application. The variable is 1 for the answer "Yes" and 0 otherwise. It should be noted that this measure captures only observed behavior of users linked with the potential adopter and is therefore a measure of *local* social influence or social influence by peers (in analogy to local versus global network effects).

(2) Experience of active social influence: Potential adopters can experience active social influence through various channels. The distinguishing feature of active social influence is, however, that the person, who exerts the influence, does so not only by accident but deliberately passes on information. I capture this important characteristic by asking the respondents whether Facebook friends have ever tried to actively influence their decision to use the application by passing on information. There were four different information channels as well as the answer "No". If potential adopters received information through one of the four channels, the variable "Active influence perceived" is 1 and 0 otherwise.

Importance of network effects for benefits derived from using a product (both models)

If the use of a product or service incorporates network effects, the degree of existing externalities depends on the number of other people using the same product or service. I distinguish *local* and *global* network effects by asking respondent to indicate on a five-point Likert scale to which extent they agreed or disagreed with the following statement: „I thought my personal value of the application would be higher if more of my friends (alternatively for *global* network effects: more people) used it." The measure is included in the estimation as dummy variable that takes the value 1 if respondents indicate a "strong (5)" or "somewhat (4)" perception of network effects. The variable is 0 otherwise.

4.5.1.3 Control variables

Experience of global, passive social influence (Adoption model only): In principle, users can experience passive social influence also from observing the choices and behavior of anonymous Facebook users not linked to their profiles. In particular, Facebook makes the number of users using a certain application transparent by compiling application rankings including the number of installs. It might well be the case that the decision of potential adopters is influenced by the total number of adopters. This could be interpreted as *global* social influence as it stems from the observation of the population of Facebook users.[114] In order to control for global social influence, I chose to utilize a data set that includes daily data on the number of installations of a particular application.[115] In the survey, respondents were asked to indicate in which month they had first installed the application. If the respondent had answered the question, a monthly average of the above described data was used for respective month and application. If an answer was missing, an overall average was used for each respective application.[116]

Rogers' determinants of adoption (Adoption model only): I consider a series of variables that are adopted from commonly used items to measure the determinants of the adoption decision (Rogers 1983). All items were measured via a five-point Likert scale and respondents were asked to which extent they agreed or disagreed. Specifically, I consider the "perceived ease of use" of a product of service as well as three measures for costs that users might incur with an adoption. For this I take into account costs that relate to "privacy concerns", "opportunity costs of time" and finally a measure of "cost of profile overload" which refers to the potential cost that a user incurs if he installs too many applications which then make his profile page confusing.

Early adopter (Adoption model only) and *Opinion leadership (Active influence model only):* The importance of early adopter and opinion leaders in the decision making process of individuals was introduced by Katz & Lazarsfeld (1955) who found in a study of voting decisions that only a small fraction considered themselves being influenced by the mass media whereas most people claimed that they were above all influenced by certain individuals among their family and friends. Opinion leaders provide

---

[114] It is acknowledged that here the transition to global network effects is blurred. However, since in this study network effects are chosen to be measured by directly asking respondents to indicate their perception of network effects, this controlling effect is defined to be a passive social influence.

[115] This measure was computed from data available from the data set as described in chapter 2.

[116] 218 of 358 respondents (60.89%) did not answer the questions respective the time when they installed the application. Due to the high share of users being assigned to the mean value of adoption time, the measure is likely exhibit significantly less variance than the actual distribution of the adoption time. This caveat is acknowledged and needs to be considered in the following analysis.

their peers with information and advice, and this information triggers acceptance of the advocated position by the recipient of the opinion. The variable is built as an index based on a series of items that were taken and adapted from Sheth et al. (1999).

Familiarity (Active influence model only): This variable takes the value of 1 (0 otherwise) if the respondent has indicated that he is very familiar with the application. Due to the design of the survey that relates all questions to one specific application, I aim at controlling whether the decision to actively influence peers depends on the level of interaction and involvement with the application.

Demographics (both models): In terms of personal characteristics, I consider measures of the respondents gender (1 if "male", 0 otherwise) and age. For nationality, I include two dummies. They take the value of 1 if the respondent is from the "USA" (respectively: "Germany") and 0 otherwise. The distinction is made because the two nationalities are represented in the sample most. Also, users from the USA can be assumed to differ in their usage behavior from German users because Facebook was a rather novel service in Germany at the time of the survey.

4.5.2 Model specification

In the multivariate analyses, I attempt to link two separate decisions to the presence of social influence as well as an individual's perception of network effects. As each of those decisions, i.e. to adopt and to exert active influence, is characterized by two mutually exclusive choices, a standard discrete choice framework is used for the multivariate analysis. Similar to previous studies of technology adoption on the individual level, a Probit model is chosen to analyze the influence of a broad set of variables on the two decisions. Note that Probit models can be derived from an underlying model of utility maximization and are therefore in line with the notion that both product adoption as well as exertion of active influence occur only if the utility from doing so exceeds the associated cost.

Assume that the utility derived from active influence/ product adoptions y^* is a function of a set of characteristics X (like product features, existence of network effects, personal traits as well as the cost associated with the choice) and an individual shock or error term which is symmetrically distributed around zero with

$$y^* = X\beta + e \qquad (4)$$

β is the vector of parameters determining the strength of the influence of the characteristics. The utility derived from each choice alternative cannot be observed by the econometrician. Further, active influence and product adoption respectively occur only if the derived utility is above a certain threshold level of utility which is normalized to zero. The decision whether active influence is exerted or whether a product is adopted respectively can be observed. Let $y = 1$ if product adoption/active influence occurs, which is the case for all for $y^* > 0$, and $y = 0$ if not. The Probit model can then be derived with

$$P(y = 1 \mid X) = P(y^* > 0 \mid x) = P(e > -X\beta \mid X) = 1 - G(-X\beta) = G(X\beta) \quad (5)$$

and G(.) being the cumulative normal distribution (see (Wooldridge 2002)). An alternative choice for G(.) would be the logit function.

In the following analyses I report marginal effects from two separate Probit analyses: (i) a Probit analysis of the decision to adopt a product and (ii) a Probit analysis of the decision to exert active influence. The reported marginal effects are given by

$$\frac{\partial G(x\beta)}{\partial x_i} = G'(x\beta) \cdot \beta_i \quad (6)$$

and therefore depend on the x through G(xβ). The marginal effects reported for x_i are computed at the remaining variables' x_{-i} means.

4.5.3   Results and discussion

This section presents the results of the Probit estimations of the two models.

4.5.3.1   Adoption of new products

I first report the results regarding the determinants of the decision to adopt a given application. Table 19 contains the results from Probit estimations linking the decision to adopt a new product (yes = 1) to a number of potential determinants of product adoption. Those determinants include the variables of main interest (measures of social influence and the perception of network effects) but at the same time important control variables. The presentation and discussion of the results are based on the model reported in column (1). This specification contains all control variables as well as dummy variables for the different applications covered in the questionnaire.[117] The specifications in column (2) and (3) serve as robustness checks. The specification reported in column (2) does not include the control variables but includes the application fixed

---

[117] Application fixed effects are not reported here for reasons of brevity but can be obtained from the author upon request.

effects. The specification in column (3) does include the control variables but no application fixed effects. When looking at the results of the different specifications, it becomes apparent that the results of my preferred specification reported in column (1) are robust – both in terms of effect strength and significance level – to variations in the set of regressors.

It is the primary goal of this study to analyze whether a user's perception of social influence and network effects influences his decision to adopt an application. Turning first to the effect of social influence, the results from the multivariate analysis support the hypotheses brought forward in section 4.2. In particular, I find that users who were exposed to social influence are significantly more likely to adopt an application than users that were not: Users who experienced passive social influence (by observing friends' behavior) were 24.4% more likely to adopt an application (see column 1). Also, users that were actively approached by friends are characterized by an adoption probability that is 13.3% higher when compared to users that have not been actively approached (see column 1). Note that both effects are highly significant.

Regarding the effect of a user's perception of his network-based benefits from using an application my results are interesting as they differ across local and global network effects. While I find support for hypothesis H1-2a regarding the positive effect of the perception of local network effects, the results from the multivariate analysis do not support my expectation that global network effects increase the likelihood of adoption (hypothesis H1-2b). In fact, users that expect to benefit from an application's local network effects are 21.3% more likely to adopt that application than users that do not expect to benefit from local network effects (see column 1). On the other hand, I find no significant difference between users that expected to benefit from global network effects and those that did not.

Table 19: Results from a Probit analysis of application adoption decisions

	Estimation of adoption decision (reporting marginal effects at the mean)		
	(1)	(2)	(3)
VARIABLES	Adoption (0/1)	Adoption (0/1)	Adoption (0/1)
Passive: awareness of friends' use (0/1)	0.224**	0.304***	0.271***
	(0.107)	(0.0787)	(0.0932)
Active: invitation received (0/1)	0.133*	0.149**	0.144**
	(0.0692)	(0.0631)	(0.0662)
Benefit from local network effects (0/1)	0.213***	0.173**	0.226***
	(0.0736)	(0.0692)	(0.0706)
Benefit from global network effects (0/1)	-0.0270	0.0403	-0.0738
	(0.0877)	(0.0825)	(0.0809)
Passive: installations (in Millions)	-0.0166		-0.00389
	(0.0131)		(0.00579)
Early adopter	0.0737***		0.0633**
	(0.0252)		(0.0249)
Ease of use	0.0853**		0.0849**
	(0.0407)		(0.0400)
Privacy concern	-0.0899***		-0.101***
	(0.0240)		(0.0228)
Cost of profile overload	-0.0966***		-0.103***
	(0.0238)		(0.0238)
Cost of time	0.0177		0.0266
	(0.0248)		(0.0245)
Male (0/1)	-0.167**		-0.186***
	(0.0692)		(0.0646)
Respondent age	0.00807		0.0188
	(0.0468)		(0.0432)
Squared: respondent age	-0.000133		-0.000302
	(0.000875)		(0.000825)
USA (0/1)	-0.0467		-0.0224
	(0.0760)		(0.0737)
Germany (0/1)	0.0658		0.0536
	(0.0797)		(0.0751)
Application dummies included	YES	YES	NO
Observations	356	356	356
Log-likelihood	-180.0	-215.8	-187.0
Pseudo R^2	0.269	0.123	0.241

Note: Robust standard errors in parentheses; *** p<0.01, ** p<0.05, * p<0.1; application dummies included in (1) and (2) but not displayed; not included in (3).

To summarize, I find that the likelihood that a user adopts a product is positively related to social influence (both passive and active) as well as his expectations towards the benefits derived from a product's local network effects. It is noteworthy, that these results have been obtained controlling for a set of alternative determinants of product adoption. I find weak evidence that early adopters for other products in the sense of Rogers (1983) are more likely to adopt an application on Facebook. An interpretation of this finding is that Facebook applications where relatively new at the time of the survey and thus users who generally are more likely to try out novel internet services would also be the first to install Facebook applications. My findings regarding product characteristics that influence product adoption as proposed by Rogers (1983) are in line with prior expectations. In particular, I observe strong and positive effects for the personal benefit that is derived from adopting and using an application as well as for its expected ease of use. Both effects are highly significant. On the other hand, the likelihood of product adoption is significantly decreased by privacy concerns as well as the cost which is associated with profile overload. I include this measure to analogously capture Roger's determinant of complexity incurred as a consequence of adopting a product. No significant effects for opportunity cost of time are found. Again, those findings are robust across the different specifications presented in columns (1) and (3). Regarding the demographic characteristics of the users surveyed I find only one significant effect: Male respondents are between 17% to 19% less likely to adopt a product compared to their female counterparts.

4.5.3.2   Active influence of peers

The analysis of the previous section showed that the likelihood of product adoption is significantly higher for potential adopters that experienced passive and active social influence as well as for users that expect to benefit from an application's local network effects. I now turn to the question which factors determine whether individuals choose to exert active influence on their peers.

Again, these findings have been obtained controlling for alternative determinants such as demographic user characteristics and application fixed effects. Regarding those additional determinants, I observe male users to be less likely to become active influencer. Moreover, if I do not control for application specific effects, increasing familiarity with a product raises the likelihood of becoming an active influencer. Once I control for application fixed effects, however, this effect vanishes. The other control variables, including whether the user had been actively influenced himself, have no significant effect on the likelihood of exerting active influence. Table 20 reports the results from a Probit analysis relating the influence decision to measures of perceived network effects as well as a set of control variables. Based on previous work of Henkel & Block (2008), I formulated the hypothesis that the likelihood of an individual acting as an active influencer is a function increasing in the perceived extent of network effects associated with a product (Hypothesis 2-1). Moreover, I expect that the effect of network externalities associated with a user's friends and peers, i.e. local network effects, is stronger than the effect of global network externalities (Hypothesis 2-1a).

The results provide strong support for both hypotheses. Table 20 shows that the perceived importance of local network effects has a positive and highly significant influence on the probability that an individual acts as an active influencer. Expecting to benefit from local network effects creates a strong incentive to exert active influence on friends: the likelihood of active influence increases by more than 30%. Moreover, perceived global network effects do not have a significant effect on the likelihood that users exert active social influence on the peers in the study. This is in line with the theoretical prediction of Henkel & Block (2008) who argue that the existence of local network effects creates a greater incentive to actively influence peers than global network effects.

Again, these findings have been obtained controlling for alternative determinants such as demographic user characteristics and application fixed effects. Regarding those additional determinants, I observe male users to be less likely to become active influencer. Moreover, if I do not control for application specific effects, increasing familiarity with a product raises the likelihood of becoming an active influencer. Once I control for application fixed effects, however, this effect vanishes. The other control variables, including whether the user had been actively influenced himself, have no significant effect on the likelihood of exerting active influence.

Table 20: Results from a Probit analysis of peer influence decisions

	Estimation of influence decision (reporting marginal effects at the mean)		
	(1)	(2)	(3)
VARIABLES	Influence (0/1)	Influence (0/1)	Influence (0/1)
Benefit from local network effects (0/1)	0.306***	0.302***	0.235***
	(0.0922)	(0.0900)	(0.0852)
Benefit from global network effects (0/1)	-0.0424	-0.0448	-0.0266
	(0.119)	(0.115)	(0.104)
Active: invitation received (0/1)	0.127		0.127
	(0.111)		(0.101)
Opinion leadership	0.000280		-0.0364
	(0.0522)		(0.0496)
Familiarity high (0/1)	0.145		0.185**
	(0.0942)		(0.0874)
Male (0/1)	-0.188*		-0.214**
	(0.105)		(0.0940)
Respondent age	0.0915		0.0634
	(0.0780)		(0.0726)
Squared: respondent age	-0.00157		-0.00112
	(0.00152)		(0.00145)
USA (0/1)	0.0585		0.0889
	(0.111)		(0.103)
Germany (0/1)	-0.0185		-0.0138
	(0.114)		(0.105)
Application dummies included	YES	YES	NO
Observations	168	168	168
Log-likelihood	-91.37	-96.47	-100.5
Pseudo R^2	0.207	0.163	0.128

Note: Robust standard errors in parentheses; *** $p<0.01$, ** $p<0.05$, * $p<0.1$; application dummies included in (1) and (2) but not displayed; not included in (3).

4.6   Chapter summary

One of the most pervasive determinants of an individual's behavior is the influence of those around him. However, the role of social environment in individual decision making regarding product adoption is still poorly understood. Thus, the aim of this chapter was to examine different facets of social environment on two distinct, economic decisions: the adoption and the promotion of novel products. In particular, it further specified the abstract term "social environment" by distinguishing between social influence, which can be exerted both actively and passively, and network externalities, which are a consequence of both the technical features of the product and the behavior of other people. Results from the empirical study on applications on Facebook's networking service suggest that this distinction is indeed meaningful. Specific types of social influence do significantly contribute to explaining the two above mentioned decisions.

With regard to the adoption decision, the empirical results based on an online survey of Facebook users indicate a significant, strong and positive effect of the social environment on an individual's behavior. Users who have been pointed to an application by their peers are more likely to adopt it than users who have not. The marketing literature refers to this effect as word-of-mouth which was found to increase the probability of purchase in a variety of settings (Arndt 1967; Harrison-Walker 2001; Hill et al. 2006). The role of passive social influence has been found to be an even more important determinant of an individual's adoption decision. Furthermore, I find significant influence of local network effects on the adoption decision. Finally, I find significant effects for a series of control variables such as the characteristics of the application (Rogers 1983). These effects are in line with theoretical prediction and contribute to my confidence in the survey design and measurements.

With regard to a user's decision to promote an application or not, my findings are consistent with previous research. While the perception of global network effects does not significantly influence an individual to actively recommend an application to peers, the perception of local network effects does have a significant, strong positive effect. This is in line with the theoretical prediction of Henkel & Block (2008). Users in small, local networks are inclined to pull the remaining non-users of the product into using the service. In addition to those effects, I observe male users to be less likely to become active influencers.

The findings of this study support the argumentation for an increased likelihood of bandwagon processes in a socially embedded context such as Facebook's social networking service. Social influence, both passive and active, are dominant determinants of a user's decision to adopt an application on the platform. Since some applications in addition seem to exhibit increasing returns the more friends are using it, positive and reinforcing processes are likely. As a consequence, the findings suggest that these social processes significantly contribute to the skewed distribution of application success. This supports the argument for a "superstar effect" (Rosen 2011) as important driver of application demand. Indeed, Boudreau & Hagiu (2010) suggest that platform operators like Facebook regulate the market for applications such that winner-takes-all outcomes arise in niches to incentivize developers to contribute high quality applications.

These findings also bear relevance for the management and marketing of products and services. The findings are particularly relevant in an internet-enabled context. The strength of the internet since inception was to make information easily shareable and available. In the marketing of products, this information relates to both the purposeful recommendation of products (active influence) as well as the ability to observe behavior of peers (passive influence).

The results furthermore point to the importance of identifying and incentivizing existing users to pass on product recommendations. The descriptive analysis of this chapter showed that users primarily use channels that are deeply integrated with the functionality of the application or Facebook service. This implies that managers need to consider and integrate word-of-mouth functionality already during the product development phase. Utilizing the existing user base becomes a taunting task once the product is developed and marketed and does not make recommending easy and without friction. This is particularly true since the analysis showed that users are primarily motivated by intrinsic incentives. Extrinsic motives such as bonus points to use for the application were identified to be less important. The results also showed that a distinction between peers and the overall user base is important when designing products and marketing strategies that rely on the positive, reinforcing process of direct network effects. Both the decision to adopt and to promote an application is influenced by a user's perception of local but not global network effects.

The study examines a rather novel phenomenon and exhibits some limitations that provide room for further research. It was the deliberate aim to conceptually capture the difference between social influence and network effects and to include both determinants in a model of product adoption. Future research could measure constructs in more depth. A limitation of this study is the cross-sectional approach. Further research could try to capture the product's life-cycle and explore the dynamics of adoption and promotion activities. Finally, the research provides insights into the dissemination of applications on Facebook Platform. While I am confident that these findings are applicable to a variety of internet-enabled contexts, further research should examine to what extent the results also hold in an environment that is characterized by higher friction and costs of interaction between users and in which consumers incur costs in form of prices.

5   Interdependencies between applications

5.1   Chapter overview

The descriptive analysis of Facebook's platform for applications in section 3.3.2 showed that application success, with regard to application usage, is highly skewed. Economists are interested in highly concentrated markets because of the inherent risk of welfare loss due to inefficiencies such as the lack of incentives for producers to market products (in this dissertation: Facebook applications) that only few consumers appreciate. Skewed market outcomes are most commonly explained by differences in product quality and social effects in consumption. Another potential cause, the consumers' lack of information about available alternatives (Hendricks & Sorensen 2009), is the focus of this dissertation and is examined in more detail in this chapter.

In order to study the role of information on the adoption and usage of applications, I examine the interdependence of usage between applications of the same developer in more detail.[118] Specifically, I analyze the impact of the launch of a new application on the usage of applications which were released previously by the same developer. The event of the launch of the new application is assumed to be an occasion for users to discover this new as well as the developer's earlier applications. The discovery, i.e. receiving information about, previous applications because of the new application is in the following referred to as information spillover. Information spillovers, as already defined in section 1.3.3.1, occur when consumers discover and learn about a product because of their discovery or consumption of another product of the same producer. In the following, I focus on the analysis of *backward* spillovers which describe the process that consumers learn about products *previously* released to the one that they are initially consuming.[119] In the following section 5.2, I will describe the mechanism of information spillovers for the case of Facebook applications.

---

[118] Recall that there exist developers that built and launched more than one application in the period of this study. These developers are referred to as portfolio developers. The following analysis builds on the empirical study in chapter 3 which examined developer portfolios and the time between the launch of two applications.

[119] Recall that *forward* spillovers conversely refer to the process in which consumers who already have a product and through it learn about newly released products from the same producer.

The main study on information spillovers between products is the work by Hendricks & Sorensen (2009) on spillovers between music albums based on data prior to the dominance of digital music and the distribution of albums via the internet. In the discussion of their findings, the authors argue that the internet may change the occurrence and magnitude of information spillovers. Now consumers gather information about products more easily and have the opportunity to sample the music before a purchase. The radio as main broadcast medium or the display of albums in brick and mortar stores do not play an equally important role for the discovery of new music. The authors expect that as a result of this easier access to information, spillovers become smaller and, thus, distribution of success less skewed. This again may lead to a welfare gain through an increased variety of albums in the market.

Recently, the emergence of online social networks has changed the context in which cultural goods (music, movies, games, etc.) and many other digital goods are discovered and consumed even more. Forrester Research estimates that people in the US create 256 billion impressions of peer influence by posting comments or referrals in social networks. Of these, about 62% happen on Facebook (Bernoff 2010). This means that consumers increasingly experience the internet as strongly socially embedded environment: activities by peers are highly visible in form of "hit lists" (Oestreicher-Singer & Sundararajan 2008) or News Feeds (Naaman et al. 2010) and it is frictionless and often times even favorable for consumers to pass on information to their peers (Henkel & Block 2008).[120] However, the body of literature on the consequences of internet-enabled environments and online social networks on market outcomes is still scarce.

The following empirical study contributes to this new and emerging stream of literature by performing, to the best of the author's knowledge, the first analysis on information spillovers for digital goods and, specifically, Facebook applications. I proceed as follows. The next section 5.2 discusses the context of information spillovers on Facebook Platform. The mechanism of the discovery of Facebook applications is revisited and examined with a focus on interdependencies between two or more applications within a developer's portfolio. The following section 5.3 introduces the empirical

---

[120] Chapter 4 of this dissertation provides an analysis of such social context for the case of Facebook. Other studies have begun to develop algorithm-based approaches of systems that recommend suitable and attractive applications to users based on the popularity of the application, the user's preferences but also the extent to which his peers are using it (Li & Hsiao 2009).

model used to measure demand for applications in the weeks before and after the launch of a new application. The section describes the methodology of treatment effects which was chosen following Hendricks & Sorensen (2009). It also describes the data. Section 5.4 presents and discusses the findings. The chapter closes in section 5.5 with a summary and a discussion of further research questions.

5.2   Information spillovers on the Facebook platform

The previous section established that the discovery and consumption of digital products has changed with the emergence of online social networks. The following examines and discusses the mechanism of information spillovers for the specific case of Facebook applications. After I first revisit the general discovery of new applications, I focus on the interdependence between applications.

With more than 20,000 Facebook applications to choose from, users face an overwhelming set of choices which is impossible to evaluate in depth.[121] While this situation is common for both digital and physical cultural goods (Anderson 2006), the way in which users deal with this variety of applications and discover new ones is very different than the arguably predominant source of information that the radio was for the music industry (Hendricks & Sorensen 2009). The findings of chapter 4.4 show that the channels through which users become aware of applications has become more varied and predominantly influenced by a user's peers.[122] Only around 3% of users responding to the survey indicated that they found the application by themselves, while the vast majority discovered applications either through active invitation by requests and other interaction attempts (about 47%)[123] or through observing that a friend was using it (about 45% of the respondents). Furthermore, respondents who indicated that they observed usage by friends were three times more likely to have found an applica-

---

[121] By end of 2010, there were more than 2 million developers with applications. See Facebook (2011c) for Facebook's site on up-to-date statistics on the platform as well as overall membership and usage.

[122] Note that the survey was online for two weeks in February 2008 and, thus, in the middle of the period that is studied here (September 2007 – June 2008). It is also at the time of the significant changes that Facebook introduced the policy changes that affected the way developers were able to contact users via the News Feed. See section 0 for a discussion of these changes.

[123] Note that this had been exploited by developers to an extent that prompted Facebook to introduce the changes; see section 0.

tion while browsing that friend's profile page as opposed to receiving a notification in the News Feed.

The latter, as a form of broadcast medium, is the channel that is the closest equivalent to the role of the radio for the discovery of music. Note, however, that there are important differences in this comparison as well. Facebook's News Feed compiles activities and events from one's friends, thus having a significantly stronger social component than classical radio. As a consequence, messages received via the News Feed can be assumed to be more personalized and relevant. It can be argued that this makes the News Feed a more effective channel for discovery. This also applies for distribution, since there is no break in the adoption process. Applications can be installed (i.e. the equivalent of purchased) immediately and without friction compared to compact disk music albums for which consumers had to go to a brick and mortar store to buy. This decrease in transaction costs can also be assumed to exist for the active search for new applications. Instead of the trip to the store to search for and purchase new music, Facebook users can simply browse the Facebook directory of applications which is easily accessible from within the online networking service. The application directory is searchable and different lists with regard to category or popularity facilitate finding new applications.[124] Applications could also be discovered via search engines like Google (the Facebook directory is public and is indexed by search engine crawlers).

Another source of information about new products comes from the direct access that producers have to their customers. If a user, for example, has previously used another application released by the developer, he can be targeted and contacted directly if a new application is being released. Developers can also contact users indirectly through messages about a friend's activity with an application. These messages are automatically generated and broadcasted and observed by many users.

The focus of this study is whether usage of previous applications increases (or decreases) if new applications are launched by the same developer. The following conceptualizes two different cases in which this backward spillover may occur.

In the first case, users have not interacted or installed the prior, "catalog" application. Rather, they became aware of a new application for the first time, for example through

---

[124] Note, however, that the survey of Facebook users (see chapter 4.4) shows that only very few (less than 2% of the respondents) got to know the last application they installed via the directory. The predominant mechanisms are recommendations and invitations from friends as well as discovering applications on the profile of friends (see above).

their social network. After they install and start using the new application, they "open" themselves to receiving information (e.g. via advertising on the application's canvas page) or are actively searching themselves. If they discover other, previous applications released by the developer that they like, they may install and use these.[125]

In the second case, users already have installed and used an application. Here, users discover a new application by the developer through their social network (see above). Or, alternatively, they get to know the application directly through the same developer in form of a message or advertising on the prior application's canvas page. If the user likes the new application, he installs and starts using it. Activated by their attention to the new application, they may "re-discover" and increase usage of the prior application. In this case, the backward spillover is better described as an "attention spillover" rather than an "information spillover" which relates to users discovering an application for the first time.[126]

The distinction between these two cases is necessary because the success measure is for repeated use - not one time purchases. This process is not uncommon for digital products which are monetized indirectly by advertising or directly via subscriptions.[127] Products are monetized by "usage", not one time purchase. As a consequence, "reactivation" is a comparably important motive. Both are significantly more complex than in the case described by Hendricks & Sorensen (2009).

What is the impact that these changes in the market environment and the different mechanisms have on the occurrence and the "strength" of spillover effects? The answer is ambiguous. On the one hand, Hendricks & Sorensen (2009) argue that spillovers decrease if the internet replaces the radio as an information source since it is likely to make it easier for consumers to sample different options. On the other hand, it

---

[125] Note that this information spillover works both backward and forward. New releases can be advertised or even pre-announced on the canvas page of an application that the user is already actively using.

[126] Note that in the "re-discovering" case, it is not necessary that the user actually installs and uses the new application for the usage of the prior application to increase. The signal of a new application suffices. In fact, this mechanism is not different in the case of music (as examined by Hendricks & Sorensen (2009)). The backward spillover from hearing about a new song on the radio is likely to also induce people who already bought the prior album to listen to it again. While this spillover effect is not accounted for in commercial terms in the traditional industry model of sales in brick and mortar stores, it is relevant for business models in the digital music industry in which consumption of music is monetized directly or indirectly.

[127] These monetization strategies are also employed for digital music.

can be argued that spillovers increase because producers or developers now have the opportunity to approach their users directly. In the case of Facebook applications, this means that other applications can be promoted on the available screen space of applications that users already have installed.[128] The above discussed importance of social channels, however, is likely to increase concentration of application use because it is increasingly easy for consumers to coordinate their preferences.

Due to this ambiguity and the lack of previous theoretical and empirical research in the field in general and for the case of Facebook applications specifically, it is difficult to bring forward a definitive hypothesis regarding the existence and effect of spillovers in this case. As a consequence, the following empirical analysis is of exploratory nature. The approach in which I perform the analysis is introduced in the following exploratory section.

5.3 Empirical approach

This section introduces the empirical approach of measuring backward spillovers between applications. The following section 5.3.1 covers the data by describing the sample. Section 5.3.2 first introduces the methodology of treatment effect studies and how it is implemented in the setting of this research project. The specifications of the estimations are defined and explained in section 5.3.3.

5.3.1 Data

In order to measure and analyze information spillovers, I constructed a data set consisting of the usage histories of a sample of 452 developers of Facebook applications in the period from September 2007 until June 2008.[129] I included developers who launched at least two applications during the sample period. The resulting sample of 1,087 applications covers a variety of categories of applications (see Figure 15). The

---

[128] It is not possible to control for the role of banner advertising on Facebook or third-party websites for the respective application. However, this form of advertising can be assumed to be less important in this study. First, advertising of this form was not popular and developed at the time of the study (less than 1% of the respondents indicate that they got to know an application from an advertisement). And second, since it is the more costly alternative (note that banner advertising has to be bought from Facebook versus the free-of-charge use of the application canvas space) developers are inclined to first utilize this form of cross promotion.

[129] The sample is based on the data described in chapter 2. Refer to section 3.2 for a description of the steps taken to construct the sample from the full data set.

highest represented categories are "Just for Fun" with 308 (28.33%), "Gaming" with 125 (11.50%) and "Dating" with 73 (6.72%) applications.[130] Other categories like "Classifieds", "Filesharing", or "Video" are represented with less than ten applications.

There are 183 developers of whom I have data on three application launches during the sample period and 269 developers for whom I observe only two launches.[131] Table 21 summarizes various aspects of the data. I describe important features of the data in the following. Panel A shows the distribution of the applications' launch dates, separated by launch order. The median launch of a developer's first application is calendar week 45 in 2007, i.e. nine weeks into the start of the sample period (week 36 in 2007). The last developers in the sample launched their first application in late March 2008.[132]

The sample is characterized by a considerable heterogeneity in active usage of applications.[133] Panel B contains the summary statistics for the total accumulated application usage (during the time of the sample period). The sample includes large developers like Coolapps.com (with its application "Owned!"; total accumulated usage of 11.6 million users), or Chainn Inc. with the applications "Spark" (4.2 million users) and "Social Profile" (3.3 million users). Most applications, however, only have moderate usage during the sample period with more than 250 applications having less than 2,000 active users during their entire lifetime. There are no strong differences in total accumulative usage between the different releases (see differences of the median between applications 1, 2 and 3 of Panel B).[134] This is surprising because an earlier release gives an application more time to amass usage. A likely explanation for this finding is

---

[130] For 211 (19.41%) applications, developers did not assign a category. These applications are denoted "missing" in the data. Table 30 in the appendix lists the detailed frequency distribution of categories.

[131] While data is available on whether a developer launches additional applications after the sample period, it was not included in the data (following Hendricks & Sorensen (2009)). Due to the rather short time that elapses between application launches (see description below) in relation to the overall sample period, it is unlikely that a large portion the developers did launch an additional application.

[132] This restriction was imposed by the sample selection criteria of section 3.2.

[133] This confirms the findings of section 3.3 in which different usage metrics for applications and developers were analyzed.

[134] The average first application has a total of about 10,000 users (median; mean: 141,960 users), the average third application attracted 7,800 users (median; mean: 113,780 users) and, thus, more than the second release with 6,900 users (median; mean: 95,120 users).

the rather short time between application launches (see below). Also, Facebook grew strongly in the sample period, giving later applications a larger market to address.[135]

Figure 15: Application categories for sample for information spillover analysis

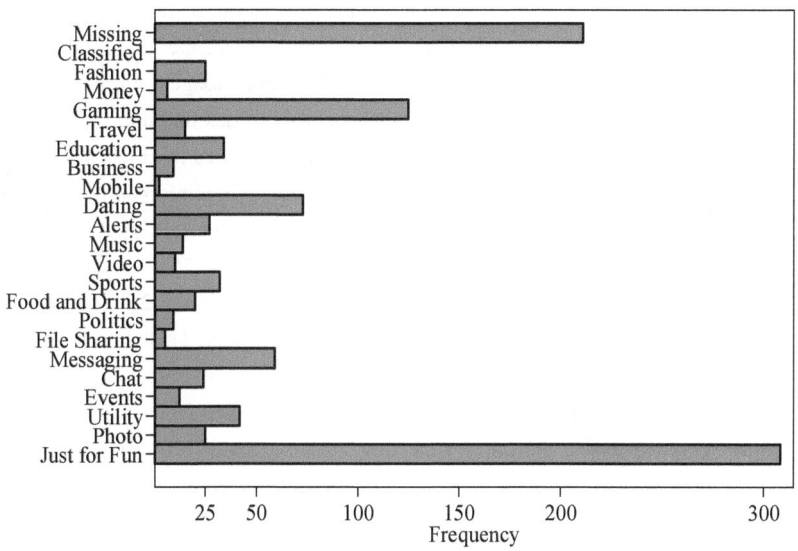

Source: own calculation.
Figure plots the frequency distribution of categories of 1,087 applications in the sample.

The data in Panel B presents accumulated usage of the entire time that an application is in the sample. In order to make this metric of success more comparable, I also computed accumulated usage for the first four and twelve weeks, respectively (see Panels C and D). The summary statistics confirm the picture that was presented above. Again, usage does not differ strongly after twelve weeks. Applications which are released third accumulate the most users with, on average, around 6,000 users (median; mean: 65,900 users). The same is true for accumulated usage after four weeks. This appears

---

[135] Note that in parallel to the growth in number of overall users, the number of applications increased as well. However, due to the skewed distribution of success among applications, the vast majority of the new applications never achieved relevant usage. These "irrelevant" applications are excluded from the sample (see section 3.2).

to support the notion that it was easier to gain users for applications that were released later on.

In the following, I analyze whether usage over time is concentrated early in an application's lifetime, i.e. in the first few weeks. I am also interested in the time until the usage of each application peaks (Panels E and F present the summary statistics). Usage appears to be rather evenly distributed over time, at least during the first twelve weeks: the usage of the first four weeks amounts to about 37% of the usage of the first 12 weeks (median of all applications; see panel E). However, usage of third releases is on average more front-loaded than earlier releases. This means that the portion of usage of the first four weeks is higher for applications that launched third when compared to first applications (compare 42% vs. 33%). This picture is reinforced by the findings that are summarized in panel F. They indicate that usage typically peaks after around four weeks (median; mean: 7.1 weeks) and that more than 25% of the applications reach their peak already in the second week. On the other hand, 25% of the applications peak after nine weeks or some only in their 40th week. This suggests that, even though the majority reaches the peak early, usage paths exhibit heterogeneity. In some cases I do not observe a peak in usage which means that these applications are continuously growing during the time of the study. An explanation for a sustained growth can be seen in network or social effects that increase the attractiveness of an application over time or as more people use it (see section 1.3.2 for a description of reinforcing mechanisms in the usage of applications).

These findings can be seen as a first hint for spillovers between applications. On the one hand, the higher concentration of overall usage in the first weeks for the third application suggests forward spillovers between applications: the installed base of previously launched applications is utilized after the release of a new application. On the other hand, the sustained growth of applications may also be explained by backward spillovers. With the launch of a new application, attention may be re-directed to previous applications. Or it may even lead to the new discovery and adoption of these applications. This univariate analysis, however, does not allow a precise interpretation. As a consequence, a dedicated methodology to isolate spillovers effects needs to be developed; the approach taken in this dissertation will be described in the following section 5.3.2.

Table 21: Summary statistics of applications in the sample

	N	Mean	SD	Percentile			Min	Max
				0.25	0.5	0.75		
				A. Week of application launch				
Application 1	452	2007w46	7	2007w40	2007w45	2007w50	2007w36	2008w12
Application 2	452	2007w51	7	2007w45	2007w50	2008w4	2007w37	2008w14
Application 3	183	2007w51	7	2007w46	2007w50	2008w4	2007w38	2007w15
				B. Total accumulated usage (in '000)				
Application 1	452	141.96	530.95	2.39	10.15	48.6	0.21	7864.76
Application 2	452	95.12	626.83	2.20	6.91	31.51	0.23	11582.3
Application 3	183	113.78	335.84	2.56	7.75	60.20	0.32	2507.39
Overall	1087	117.74	547.36	2.31	8.23	40.05	0.21	11582.3
				C. Accumulated usage in first 12 weeks (in '000)				
Application 1	452	67.86	224.77	1.26	5.17	27.81	0.11	3251.78
Application 2	452	46.24	216.02	1.38	4.67	20.50	0.09	3067.11
Application 3	183	65.90	200.88	1.53	6.02	39.08	0.24	1540.32
Overall	1087	58.55	217.32	1.35	4.87	23.53	0.09	3251.78
				D. Accumulated usage in first 4 weeks (in '000)				
Application 1	452	17.94	63.11	0.45	1.4	6.7	0.04	734.73
Application 2	452	12.39	37.82	0.45	1.59	6.0	0.01	391.53
Application 3	183	23.53	70.58	0.55	2.21	16.46	0.02	588.3
Overall	1087	16.57	55.67	0.46	1.52	7.68	0.01	734.73
				E. First 4 weeks / First 12 weeks usage				
Application 1	452	0.37	0.22	0.19	0.33	0.51	0	0.93
Application 2	452	0.41	0.23	0.24	0.39	0.58	0	0.98
Application 3	183	0.44	0.22	0.27	0.42	0.57	0	0.98
Overall	1087	0.40	0.23	0.23	0.37	0.56	0	0.98
				F. Peak usage week				
Application 1	452	7.57	7.37	2	5	10	1	40
Application 2	452	6.52	6.97	2	4	8	1	36
Application 3	183	5.94	6.32	2	4	7	1	33
Overall	1087	6.86	7.06	2	4	9	1	40
				G. Weeks between launches				
Application 1, 2	452	4.69	4.32	2	3	6	1	22
Application 2, 3	183	3.80	3.49	1	2	5	1	19

Finally, panel G lists the time elapsed between application launches. On average, the second application follows the first one after three weeks (median; mean: 4.69 weeks). The shortest time is one week, the longest as long as 22 weeks. The elapsed time between the launch of the second and third application is slightly shorter, with a median of two weeks and a mean of 3.8 weeks. Figure 16 illustrates the highly skewed distribution of elapsed time between releases. Almost 25% of the second releases follow the first after one week and another 20% after two weeks. This confirms the findings of the previous analysis of developer portfolios (see section 3.5) that applications, while there is some variation, generally follow closely after each other. This has important implications for the empirical method that is used for measuring the spillovers. The methodology of treatment effects is introduced in the following section. Here I will return to the importance of the short time between application launches.

Figure 16: Time elapsed between application launches

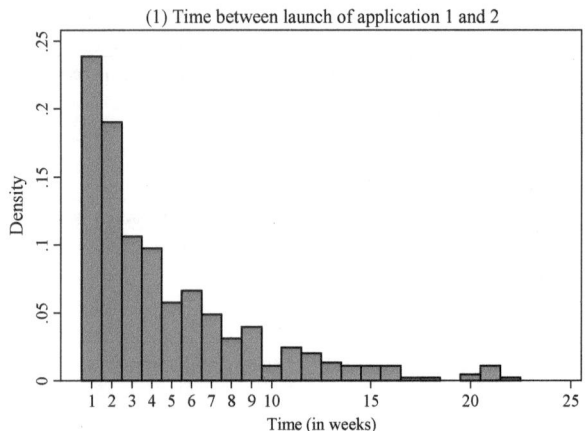

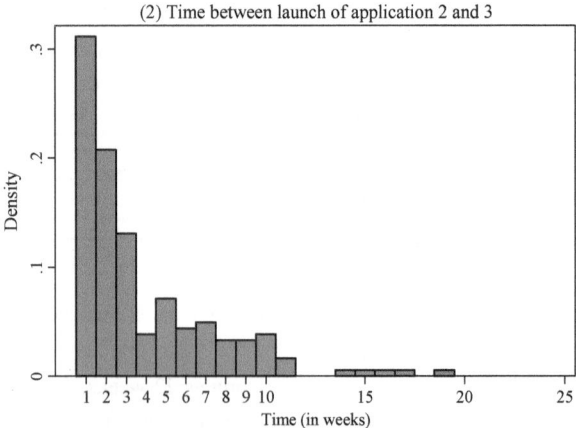

Note: (1) is based on 452 applications. (2) is based on 183 applications.

5.3.2 Methodology

I am interested in the spillovers between applications within one developer's portfolio. In order to analyze this, I follow the empirical approach taken by Hendricks & Sorensen (2009) to measure backward spillovers between artists' albums. Their approach is adapted from the literature on treatment effects.[136] This strand in the microeconometric literature provides a statistical framework for the estimation of causal parameters based on counterfactuals (Cameron & Trivedi 2005). The framework, in ideal settings, is characterized by a considerable simplicity of econometric methods. It also typically focuses on fewer causal parameters than traditional econometric approaches which aim at simultaneously modeling all structural parameters.

In economics, the term treatment (or event) is used very broadly and usually encompasses variables whose impact on some outcome is the object of study. This dissertation aims at analyzing the impact of the launch of a new application on Facebook on the usage of a developer's prior applications in their portfolio.[137] In the following, the framework is introduced in more detail and applied to the empirical case of this dissertation.[138]

The framework assumes that every element in the target population is potentially exposed to the respective treatment. In the case of this study, this implies that every application may experience the event of an additional, newer application being launched by the same developer.[139] In the model, the treatment is denoted by a categorical variable D that takes the values 1 and 0, respectively, when treatment is or is not received. Since the receipt and nonreceipt of treatment are mutually exclusive states for each application i, only one of the two measures is available for any given i (the unavailable measure being the counterfactual). The effect of the cause D on the outcome of individual i is measured by $(y_{1i} - y_{0i})$ which is the difference in the outcomes of the treated (i.e. y_{1i}) and untreated (i.e. y_{0i}) groups of applications. The average causal effect of $D_i = 1$ compared to $D_i = 0$ is measured by the average treatment effect (ATE):

---

[136] For a summary of the method, see Wooldridge (2002). The method is also referred to as program evaluation or treatment evaluation.

[137] In Hendricks & Sorensen (2009), analogously, the objective is to measure the impact that the release of a new album (i.e. the treatment) has on the albums previously released by the same artist.

[138] The description follows section 2.7.1 in Cameron & Trivedi (2005).

[139] In the following, the general term "element" will be interchangeably used with the term "application", which is specific to the empirical case of this dissertation.

$$\text{ATE} = E[y \mid D = 1] - E[y \mid D = 0] \tag{7}$$

where expectations are with respect to the probability distribution over the target population.

The setup of the estimation of ATE-type parameters requires an experimental approach with two important requirements. First, in order to yield consistent estimates, the treatment must be assigned randomly before outcomes of treated cases are compared with the set of nontreated cases. Because random assignment of treatment is generally not feasible or rarely occurs in economics, the estimation is based on observational data generated under nonrandom treatment assignment. In this case, the consistent estimation of ATE is threatened by several complications that include possible correlation between the outcomes and treatment, omitted variables, and endogeneity of the treatment variable.

As a consequence, it is necessary to determine whether the assignment is uncorrelated with the attributes of treated applications. Specifically, it needs to be tested whether the time between application launches is determined by the success or usage pattern of the previous application. The analysis of developer portfolios in 3.5 of this dissertation provides the necessary insights. The analysis estimates time between application launches with Cox proportional hazard models that include various application and developer characteristics as covariates. The results show that the time between application launches is unrelated (i.e. insignificant) to the previous application's success (measured by the first four weeks accumulated usage). The results on the relationship between launch-timing and the previous application's growth rate are not conclusive. The effect is either insignificant or very small (positive). I conclude that the fundamental assumption of random assignment of treatment can be sufficiently asserted in order to employ the treatment effect method in this study.[140]

These findings are consistent with the results reported by Hendricks & Sorensen (2009).[141] In their study, the time it takes to release an artist's new album is essentially

---

[140] See section 3.5.4 for a description of the specification as well as the results of the estimation of the time elapsed between application launches. The results uncover significant effects like frequency of updates to the application's directory page or developer experience. These effects will be controlled for by estimating the usage interdependence between applications with application-developer fixed effects.

[141] See Hendricks & Sorensen (2006) for tables of the results of their implementation of the Cox proportional hazard model. Note that I also computed the results for a similarly re-

independent of the success of the prior album (as measured by first six months' sales) and of its decline rate. An explanation for this finding, the authors argue, may be that the time between album releases is primarily determined by the artist's creative process (i.e. writing and producing a new album). This process entails ideas, coordination and effort, which are subject of the vagaries of the artist's moods and incentives. A similar case can be made for the development of Facebook applications.

The second requirement for setting up an experimental framework that allows the use of the treatment effects methodology relates to defining and identifying the two groups of applications, treated and non-treated, that shall be compared. Causal statements can only be made if the counterfactual can be clearly stated and made operational.

I follow Hendricks & Sorensen (2009) by including separate indicators for successive weeks of treatments. This set of indicators is referred to as the treatment window and consists of a total of twelve weeks (denoted by their respective indicators). The treatment window covers the period of 16 weeks. This is shorter than the period of 30 weeks that Hendricks & Sorensen (2009) include in the treatment window for music albums. Since the overall time structure is significantly shorter in the case of Facebook applications (i.e. the sample period and the life-time of an application), this shorter window is justified and is in fact relatively longer than the related study. It is important to note that the treatment window spans from four weeks before and eight weeks after the launch of the next application.[142] This allows me to capture effects that occur prior to the launch and control whether the effect from the launch of the new application diminishes (or even reverses) over time.

The two groups of applications are also separated by carefully defining the time variable in the panel data set. For each application, a time variable t counts the weeks since the application's launch (its "lifetime"), not calendar time. The twelve indicators of the treatment window, thus, identify treated and non-treated applications for each week of the application's lifetime. This implies that an "indicator t" set to 1 groups applications for which the next application has entered t weeks earlier (or later) in their lifetime. If

---

duced model (compared to the extended model that was estimated in section 3.5.4). The results are presented in Table 30 and Table 31 in the appendix. The results are qualitatively and quantitatively not different from the ones described above.

[142] In the results, the indicators for the weeks before the launch of the next application are denoted by -4, -3, etc. The indicator for the week in which the following application is launched is denoted by 0. The weeks after the launch are denoted 1, 2, 3, etc.

"indicator t" is set to 0, the application has not experienced the "treatment" of the launch of the next application in that specific period.

In addition to this separation, a sampling decision ensures that in any given t, treated applications are compared with not yet treated applications. For this, applications are included in the sample only until the last period of the treatment window. Observations on usage after that window are not used in the estimation. In the estimation (see the specification of the panel regression in section 5.3.3), the indicator, thus, captures the average effect on usage of a launch of the next application in the respective period.

5.3.3 Specification

This section specifies how usage differences between already treated and not yet treated applications are measured. The three treatment episodes of interest are estimated separately. In each estimation, y_{it} denotes the logarithm of active usage of application i in period t.[143] Using the logarithm assumes that treatment effects are proportional, not additive. This specification is chosen because usage of applications is highly skewed. It also captures some of the nonlinearity that can be expected of the average treatment effect (Hendricks & Sorensen 2009).

Based on the panel data set, a panel regression estimation is chosen. This has the advantage of increased precision of the estimator when compared to a cross-sectional estimation. Also, when using the fixed effects model, it allows for unobserved individual heterogeneity that may be correlated with regressors. The fixed effects estimator measures the association between individual-specific deviations of the dependent variable from its time-averaged value. It is an adequate choice in this setting, since I am only interested in the coefficients of the indicator variables that define the treatment window. The other, unobserved regressors are captured by the fixed effects and treated as "nuisance parameters" (Cameron & Trivedi 2005). As a consequence, I specify the following regression model to be estimated in the following section:[144]

---

[143] Note that, for each application, t indexes time since the application's launch, not calendar time.

[144] The implementation of the model in the statistical software Stata follows Cameron & Trivedi (2009).

$$y_{it} = \alpha_0 + \alpha_i + \lambda_t + \sum_{s=-3}^{8} \beta_s I_{it}^s + \varepsilon_{it} \qquad (8)$$

where α_i is the developer-application fixed effect and λ_t are time dummies. The treatment window is included by the Is which are indicators equal to one if the launch of developers i's new application was s weeks away from period t. β_s measures the new application's usage impact in week s of the treatment window ($t = 0$ corresponds to the first week in which the new launch takes place).

This specification computes the difference in the average usage of, for example, application 1 between developers in treatment period s and developers who are not treated for each period. The differences are then averaged across the time periods. The stochastic error ε_{it} is assumed to be heteroskedastic across i (some developers' usage is more volatile than others')[145] and autocorrelated within i (random shocks to a developer's usage are persistent over time). The time dummies (λ_t) allow for flexible decay path of usage. It is, however, implicitly assumed that the shape of this decay path is the same across albums. Although differences in the level of demand are captured by the developer-application-fixed effects, differences in the shape of applications' sales paths are necessarily part of the error (ε). In the next section, I present the results of the different estimations.

5.4 Results and discussion

In this section, I discuss the results from the estimations that measure spillovers between Facebook applications. Because of the setup of the estimations (they include indicator variables for the 16 weeks of the treatment window), the number of reported coefficients is large. As a consequence, I present the estimates graphically.[146] Figure 17 shows the coefficients (i.e. betas) along with 95% confidence bands of the above described specification performing a fixed-effects panel regression.[147] The first panel contains the first application when treated by entry of the second application, the second panel application 1 when treated by entry of application 3, and the third panel applications 2 when treated by applications 3.

---

[145] In order to control for heteroskedasticity, standard errors are estimated cluster robust.

[146] In the appendix to chapter 5, I present a full table of the regression results (see Table 32).

[147] The confidence bands are based on standard errors that were computed clustered by developer-application-pair.

I begin with describing the significant results for the time after and before the launch of the new application and then turn to potential explanations for insignificant results. I discuss the findings and finally present a number of robustness checks and alternative specifications.

Results

The results indicate positive and consistent spillover effects for the first application after the entry of both application 2 and 3 (see panel 1 and 2 of Figure 17).[148] Since the dependent variable is the logarithm of usage, the coefficients can be interpreted as approximate percentage changes in usage resulting from the launch of the new application. The results indicate that this positive change is substantive. Starting in the week after the launch of the second application, usage of treated applications is by about 72% higher than usage of non-treated applications (see values at "1" of the top panel in Figure 17). In the following weeks, this effect increases to about 84% at week eight after the launch of the second application.

The graph also illustrates that the confidence bands for the coefficients expand over time. At the 5%-level, the results are significant only for about six weeks after the entry of the second application.[149] Note that significance in this context (and in the following description) refers to a coefficient whose lower 95% confidence band is above zero (zero indicates that there is no difference between treated and non-treated applications). The pattern of spillover effects from the launch of the third application on the usage of the first application follows a similar pattern (see second panel of Figure 17). In distinction to the above described pattern, the spike in the first week is less pronounced and the effect is overall not as strong and diminishes slightly until the end of the treatment window. Also, the effect is only significant (at the 5%-level) for the first four weeks after the launch of the third application.

---

[148] Note that the reference period is the fourth week prior to the launch of the following application. As a consequence, the indicator for this period is excluded from the estimation and is, consequently, missing in Figure 17.

[149] The results are, however, significant at the 10%-level throughout the treatment window (see Table 32 in the appendix to chapter 5).

Figure 17: Backward spillovers (fixed-effects estimation)

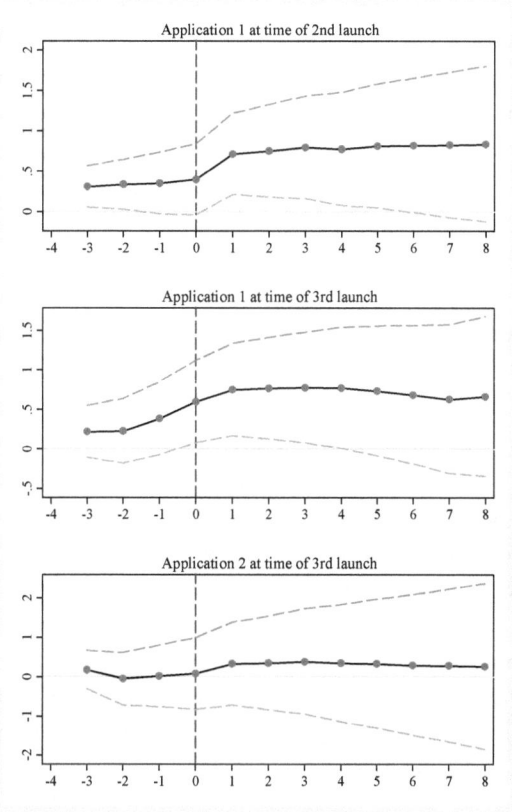

In a second step, I describe the estimation results for the time period prior to the launch of the new application (see period from -3 to 0; the launch of the second application is marked by a horizontal line in Figure 17).[150] Here, the findings for the first application are less clear than for the period after the treatment. While there is a positive effect of around 30% for application 1 in the week of and three weeks prior to the launch of the second application, it is barely significant at the 5%-level. The pattern of the effect is comparable (even though increasing before the launch week) for the spill-

---

[150] Note again that period -4 is used as reference period. Thus, the coefficient for this period is missing from the estimation results and the graph.

over from application 3 on application 1. However, the effects are insignificant at the 5%-level. The implications of this result are discussed below.

In stark contrast to the above described results, there are no significant results for a spillover effect from the launch of application 3 on the usage of application 2. The third panel of Figure 17 displays the coefficients of this estimation. While the coefficients are (slightly) positive throughout the treatment window, their standard errors are much larger than the ones in the other episodes (especially for the period after the treatment). Consequently, the effects are insignificant or statistically indistinguishable from zero. In contrast to the findings regarding the first application, which has been shown to benefit from spillover effects from both the second and the third application, this would suggest that the second and presumably later launching applications do not benefit from their following applications. Given the largely similar characteristics of the first and the second applications (see section 5.3.1 for a description), this finding is rather surprising. One explanation, especially for the wider confidence band, is the smaller number of cases on which the estimation is based. However, this does not explain the difference between the results of the second and the third panel, i.e. the impact of application 3 on the first and second application, respectively. In these estimations, the number of cases (namely 183 developer-application-pairs) is the same. Another potential reason for the missing effect could be that the usage pattern within the group of the second applications is more homogeneous than the one of the first application group. There may, for example, be a characteristic which dominates the usage path of later launching applications in a developer portfolio and which was not observed and examined in the earlier description of the data.

Discussion of findings

The above presented results suggest a number of interesting findings. Because of the lack of earlier theoretical and empirical literature on the occurrence of spillovers between Facebook applications, the effects – both in direction and strength – were unclear. It is interesting to find that there is in fact a substantive and significant positive effect that increases usage of the first application after the launch of the second and third application by up to 80% in comparison with applications that were not treated by the entry of an application. This effect is almost twice as high as the effect measured by Hendricks & Sorensen (2009) for their sample of music albums. This suggests that the lack of information about available products is even stronger in the case of

Facebook than in music. Furthermore and similar to the study on the traditional music industry, the spillover effect is surprisingly persistent.[151] In the case of Facebook applications, the effect does not decrease substantially but even increases over time for the effect of application 2 on application 1. This suggests that the mechanism causing the spillovers is of persistent nature.

The pattern of the spillover effect before the launch of the following application is also notable. In both episodes for which significant results could be obtained, i.e. the second and third application following application 1, there is a clearly identifiable spike in the week after the event. This suggests that the indicators included to mark the launch as well as the weeks before and after the event are correctly set and that the treatment effects model achieves to measure the actual difference between treated and non-treated applications. This impression is further supported by the pattern of the spillover effect before the launch of the following application. While there is a positive effect, it is clearly lower. It is only barely significant (at the 5%-level) for the spillover of application 2 on application 1 and not significant for the interaction between the third and the first application.[152]

There is an explanation for significant spillover effects on the existing application prior to the launch of the new application. In the weeks prior to the launch, a developer may be more active in the management of all his applications. For example, certain promotional activities for a new application (e.g. pre-announcements) are started before the actual launch. This is similar to the music industry, in which new releases are also promoted heavily in the weeks before the actual release. As a consequence, Hendricks & Sorensen (2009) observe positive spillovers in their study as well. The effect steadily decreases the farther away the release of the album is. Three months prior to the album release, the spillover effect is statistically inexistent. This is similar to the predominant finding of the analysis of Facebook applications and reasonable because the effect of pre-launch promotional activities is clearly less direct in the case of Facebook than it is in the case of music announced on the radio.[153]

---

[151] Note that the persistence of the effect does not necessarily imply that usage of application 1 remains steady or even increases in during that time. It rather is a relative comparison to applications that were not treated in the same period.

[152] The effect is statistically not distinguishable from zero for the spillover from the launch of application 3 on application 2 (see bottom panel of Figure 17).

[153] Insignificant results for the time prior to the launch of the next application also serve as a confirmation of the method chosen for measuring the spillovers (Hendricks & Sorensen

The existence, the strength and the source of a spillover effect is more difficult to predict in the case of Facebook applications than it is for the traditional music industry (see section 5.2). Thus, it is important to consider alternative sources and explanations than the lack of information about available applications.[154] The main alternative to information as the source of spillovers is a change in the earlier application's utility (Hendricks & Sorensen 2009). The launch of a new application may change the utility because of (1) technical, application-level complementarities or (2) social and network effects that depend on the number of users of an application.

Technical complementarities may exist if the use of the new application improves the experience of using the prior application or both applications jointly (i.e. if there exist indirect network effects between the applications (Katz & Shapiro 1985)). Since Facebook applications itself are complementary products to the social networking service of Facebook, each application is of rather limited functionality. They are not complementary systems in the sense of a video console and video games or a DVD player and DVD discs. Complementarities could, however, exist in form of learning, e.g. getting accustomed to an interface that is common across all applications of a developer. Being familiar with the interface from using the new application, the barrier to try and use the prior application may decrease. Similarly, if certain benefits (e.g. a virtual currency) are transferrable between applications, it may also increase the utility of the prior application. While these factors are possible, they are not supported by my observation of the functionality of applications on the Facebook platform during the time of the study.

The utility of an earlier application may also change if there exist social or network effects that depend on the number of users of an application. In the context of cultural goods like applications or music, such effects may arise because people like discussing these products with friends: for example, the utility from playing an application that others in the peer group have played is higher than the utility of playing the same application when no one else in the peer group has played it (Kretschmer et al. 1999; Moretti 2009). The individual-level analysis based on survey data of chapter 4 has

---

2009). In the case of music the non-existence of spillovers three months prior to the release of the next album and then the steady increase of the effect until the week of the release are a sensible path for the context. The same holds for the ambiguous results for spillovers between Facebook applications.

[154] Recall that the lack of information about the choice set is the main determinant of backward spillovers in Hendricks & Sorensen (2009).

shown that this effect does influence a user's decision to adopt an application. However, it is important to distinguish whether this effect operates within a certain application or across two applications. As a consequence, one needs to consider such effects on the developer and not the application level. The occurrence of such an effect is less likely in the context of Facebook applications.

Given that alternative explanations for the backward spillover effect found for Facebook applications are not necessarily compelling, one can conclude that the lack of information about a prior application remains the main determinant. The mechanisms discussed in section 5.2 justify this conclusion. The immense number of applications available on Facebook Platform is likely to overwhelm users. In addition to recommendations from peers (see chapter 4), developer-driven communication of new applications is a plausible source of information about earlier applications by the same developer. It is certainly a more efficient discovery mechanism than self-search.

In the following, I describe the results of several different estimations with which I test the robustness of the results that were used to derive the findings of this chapter.

Robustness of results

In order to examine the robustness of the above presented results, I implemented several alterative specifications of the estimation model. The first robustness test relates to the possible problem from the very short lag between application launches. I tested whether the results are sensitive to this data issue by computing the fixed-effects panel regression with a reduced sample. Here I excluded applications for which the time elapsed between the launches is less than three weeks. The results of this estimation are displayed in Figure 18. Here, the effect is even more clearly identified in this alternative specification than in the previously described findings. While the pattern and the strength of the effect is very close to the results based on all applications, the effect is now highly significant for the entire time period of the treatment window and for the spillover from both application 2 and 3 on the first application. The spillover effect of application 2 at time of the third application's launch also appears to be identified more precisely (see third panel of Figure 18). However, the results are still not significant at the 5%-level. This suggests that there indeed exist differences between the first and second applications.

Figure 18: Backward spillovers (fixed-effects panel, reduced sample)

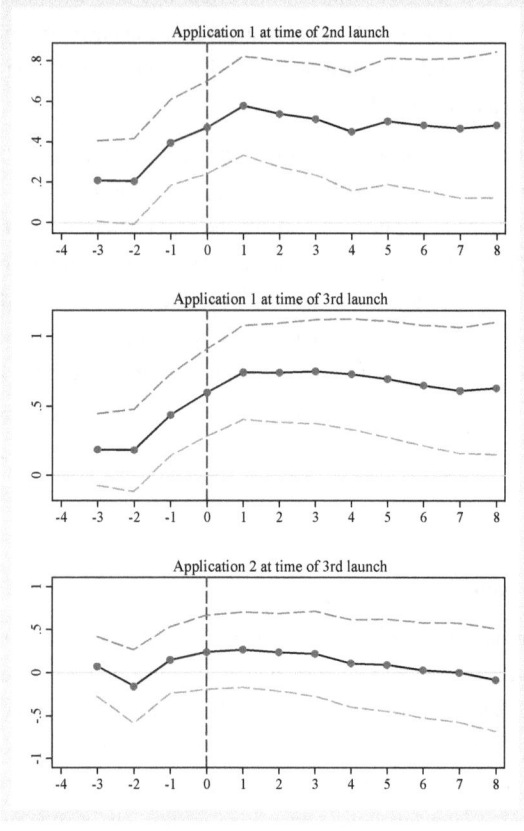

The results are also robust with regard to the use of a different estimation model. The findings from above are confirmed by the results obtained from an estimation of the full sample with a pooled ordinary least squares model (OLS) (see Table 32 in the appendix). The pattern of each spillover episode is similar to the one produced by the fixed-effects model. The strength of the effect is also comparable - with the only difference of a stronger effect for the spillover from application 3 on application 1. This suggests that there is little unobserved heterogeneity in the data which would be identified and filtered by the fixed-effects model. An additional, alternative estimation which adds relevant explanatory variables to the OLS model provided identical results.[155]

Finally, the results were tested by estimating a first-difference fixed-effects model. This specification should pick up additional, unobserved variation in the application usage pattern that was not identified by the time dummies or the fixed-effects panel estimation. The results of this estimation (see Figure 21 in the appendix) are inconclusive and not helpful in clarifying the picture. On the one hand, there are significant effects for the usage of application 1 at the time of the launch of the second application. The effect, however, is, in contrast to the results above, negative. The strength of the effect is also unreasonably strong. In the period after the launch of the next application, usage of the application is by one factor lower for treated versus non-treated applications. The negative effect more than triples until week five. Since the results for the other spillover episodes are not significant, one needs to be careful in interpreting this result. However, it becomes apparent that there may be additional, unobserved inter-temporal variation that may contribute to the spillover effect.

In conclusion, apart from results of the first-difference panel estimation, the above described robustness test confirm the findings of the main specification. Remaining caveats and limitations of this study are discussed in the following chapter summary.

5.5   Chapter summary

This section first summarizes the main findings and the contribution of this chapter. It later discusses limitations and further research questions.

Contribution

This chapter presented the first empirical analysis of information spillovers between digital products. There are important differences between digital products like Facebook applications and physical products such as compact discs of popular music albums that are sold in brick and mortar stores. The latter are the empirical context of the study by Hendricks & Sorensen (2009) which is the only work on information

---

[155] The results are presented in Figure 20 in the appendix to chapter 5. The variables included in this estimation are defined in section 3.5.3 where they were used to analyze the elapsed time between application launches. The determinants were not included in the panel regression because they were dropped by the fixed-effects estimator.

spillovers and the basis for my approach to measuring spillovers. In order to account for the differences, a new approach to conceptualizing information spillovers had to be taken. A model needs to consider that the relevant success metric is not unit sales (or revenues), but usage and time spent with the product. This implies that there is a commercially viable case in which a consumer "re-discovers" a product and uses it again because of the release of a new product. In the case of Facebook applications, it is actually not necessary that the user even installs and uses the new application for the usage of the prior application to increase. The signal of a new application may suffice. In fact, this mechanism is not different in the case of music (as examined by Hendricks & Sorensen (2009)). The backward spillover from hearing about a new album on the radio is likely to also induce people who already bought the prior album to listen to it again. While this spillover effect is not accounted for in commercial terms in the traditional industry model of sales in brick and mortar stores, it is relevant for business models in the digital music industry in which consumption of music is monetized directly or indirectly.

The properties of the conditions of markets and platforms for digital products are novel and there are no studies with empirical evidence or theoretical models for information spillovers in digital markets. Consequently, it was the objective of this dissertation to adapt the empirical approach to measuring the spillovers by Hendricks & Sorensen (2009) to the context of Facebook applications and to examine whether and to which extent information spillovers occur. The results of the analysis suggest that there are significant, positive spillover effects from the launch of an application on the usage of the prior application. Specifically, for the sample of this study, the spillover effect is clearly observable for the first application in a developer's portfolio. The effect is strongest for the launch of the second application: the results indicate a usage benefit of up to 80% compared to applications without the launch of a second application. But they are also substantive at the time of the third application's launch.[156] Somewhat surprisingly, the effect is stronger than in the case of music albums. This suggests that the lack of information about available applications is even stronger than in the case of music albums. The results are robust to variations in the estimation model and the sample. Furthermore, while alternative explanations for spillovers between applications exist, lack of information appears to be a particularly strong source.

---

[156] The estimation results for the spillover effects from the launch of the third application on the application 2 are insignificant.

Besides these original findings, they also contribute to the discussion of market structure in digital markets (Brynjolfsson et al. 2003; Fleder & Hosanagar 2009; Oestreicher-Singer & Sundararajan 2009). The findings from my study suggest that a sizeable lack of information of the available options prevails. Thus, the conclusion drawn by Hendricks & Sorensen (2009) for the traditional music industry also holds for the market for Facebook applications: market concentration is likely to be higher than desired from an economic welfare point of view. In digital markets, this effect is further strengthened because social networking and communication services enable users to coordinate easily regarding their preferences.

Finally, research on information spillovers are also of interest for strategy scholars who study competitive advantage in markets such as Facebook's platform for applications which are characterized by low barriers to entry and imitation.[157] The finding of positive effects between applications of the same developer suggests that the launch of new applications may serve as a means of maintaining and reinforcing favorable market positions. If negative effects would have been found, the launch of a new application would have diminished (or cannibalized) the usage of the overall portfolio. Nevertheless, due to the low barriers to entry, self-cannibalization may in fact be superior to being replaced by newly entering competitors. Their entry, thus, may be pre-empted by repeated, early launch of new applications from the incumbent (D'Aveni 1994; Nault & Vandenbosch 1996). This discussion shows that understanding the magnitude and sources of application usage from information spillovers is an important component of strategic decision making for developers, particularly if sustainable competitive advantage is difficult to maintain.

---

[157] See the introduction to section 3.5 for a discussion of the role of the Facebook platform API on the costs of developing an application. In addition, there is an entire ecosystem of services and offerings that aims at facilitating the development of applications. There are several books and introductory courses that allow beginners to familiarize themselves with the API (Goldman 2008; R. Wagner 2008), blogs collect daily news and analyses (Inside Facebook 2011), and there is even an investment fund dedicated for Facebook developers (fbFund 2011). Other markets with low barriers to entry that were studied by strategy researchers are the service industries, e.g. financial services (Makadok 1998; López & Roberts 2002).

Limitations and further research questions

Due to the novelty of the context and research question, this chapter's study can only be the first of number of studies in the field. Several limitations and shortcomings remain which allows for additional research.

There are some caveats with regard to the data and the results. As noted previously, the design of the crawler does not eliminate the risk that a new application is not identified and saved in the first week of its launch. However, there are no indications that this problem is substantial. Also, even though the pattern of the spillover effects suggests that the indicators used in the treatment effects model capture the effect correctly, one has to note that the robustness check of an estimation with a first-difference model produced inconclusive or slightly contradictory results. This may indicate that there remain unobserved temporal effects that were not picked up by the fixed-effects estimator and the time dummies. This issue deserves further attention but would require econometric modeling such as dynamic panel estimators (Arellano & Bond 1991) which is not in the scope of this dissertation.

The empirical study of this chapter focused on the analysis of the occurrence and the strength of information spillovers between Facebook applications. While this is a worthwhile objective, it would be valuable to investigate the sources and determinants of these spillovers in more detail. This constitutes an important opportunity for further research. One approach would be to distinguish applications based on additional characteristics (e.g. the success of each application) and analyze whether the results differ between these groups. Another natural extension to this study refers to forward spillovers that may occur from established applications to newly launched applications. This question is important for the management of applications because an existence of such spillovers would allow developers to sustain their existing user base and "transfer" them to new applications when their usage of the earlier application decreases. Hendricks et al. (2009) approach this question by developing a theoretical model of discovery of new music albums and by simulating and fitting the data to the model. A similar approach could be taken for Facebook applications; however, several adaptations would need to be implemented because the assumptions made by Hendricks & Sorensen (2009) are too restrictive or do not apply for an internet-enabled context such as Facebook's platform.

Finally, the rapidly changing market environment of digital goods provides researchers with new and developing projects. For example, Facebook Platform evolved with regard to the management of application portfolios since the study period that is the focus of this dissertation. Anecdotal evidence suggests that developers of Facebook applications in fact rely on spillovers between applications. In 2010, Facebook announced that application notifications ("stories") from users will be targeted only at friends who are also using the same application. Friends who are not users of that application will receive abstract "discovery stories." Stories on Facebook News Feed have previously been a critical promotion channel for application developers like Zynga, the market leader for Facebook games. Any change here could affect the number of new sign-ups. Cadir Lee, the CTO of Zynga, commented that developers seemed to be concerned that the changes could affect discoverability of applications (Rusli 2010). It would be interesting to investigate if the occurrence and strength of spillover effects in fact changed over time and whether this change was induced by a policy change by Facebook.

Similarly, the emergence and growing importance of technical recommender systems may also play a role in reducing the information bottleneck. Such recommender systems were pioneered by e-commerce websites such as Amazon (Oestreicher-Singer & Sundararajan 2008; Oestreicher-Singer & Sundararajan 2009; Hervas-Drane 2009). Services like Pandora and Spotify bring these mechanisms also to the music industry. In fact, there are first prototypical implementations of a recommender algorithm for Facebook applications (Li & Hsiao 2009). The economic significance of such recommender systems is exemplified by a programmer contest that was launched by the movie rental and streaming business Netflix which offered a prize of $1 million to anyone who could improve the company's system to a pre-defined degree (Lohr 2009).

6   Summary and conclusion

This chapter concludes the dissertation by summarizing the previous chapters and concluding with regard to the contribution of the findings to the discussion on market concentration in digital industries.

Summary

This dissertation set out with the observation that early studies and anecdotal evidence suggests that the distribution of success among applications on Facebook Platform is highly skewed - few large applications combine most of the usage.[158] This distribution is common in the media or entertainment industries which are often characterized by few blockbusters and a long-tail (Anderson 2006; Fleder & Hosanagar 2009). Highly concentrated markets are of interest for economist because they oftentimes bring economic welfare loss to consumers because of a decrease in product variety due to lack of incentives for producer to sell products that only appeal to few consumers (Hendricks & Sorensen 2009).

The objective of this dissertation was to analyze whether interdependencies in usage exist on the level of users and information spillovers between products. Furthermore, it was the objective to examine whether these interdependencies contribute to an increase in market concentration. I proceeded in three steps.

First, I provided an in-depth description and analysis of Facebook's platform of applications. In order to perform empirical analyses on the application and developer level, an original and extensive data set was collected. The process in which the data set was captured from Facebook's web page and prepared for statistical analysis was presented in **chapter 2**. The data set served as basis for several subsequent analyses. The descriptive analyses of **chapter 3** were then concerned in describing and analyzing additional specificities and interdependencies that exist on Facebook platform but which take a secondary role. Here, I examined the platform with regard to the supply of and demand for applications as well as the individual success of applications and developers according to different measures of application usage. I found that the distribution of success is highly skewed: few applications and developers account for most of the usage of all applications. Furthermore, a case study was presented that described an

---

[158] See Gjoka et al. (2008) and the analysis of section 3.3.

important policy change that Facebook introduced in early 2008 and which affected developers with regard to the way they were able to contact their users. The results of this analysis suggest that applications launched after the policy change were less actively used both in absolute and relative terms. It is, however, important to note that a univariate analysis, such as conducted here, does not control for many other potential explanatory determinants of application usage and success. More research is needed in order to understand the impact of the policy change in more detail. This analysis, however, illustrated the interdependence between the operator of the platform and the way developers and users interact. Finally, I studied interdependencies between applications marketed by one developer. Specifically, the analysis examined the time that elapses between the launch of two applications. The findings are surprising because there seems to be no relationship between the previous application's usage pattern and success. The findings and insights of these exploratory analyses serve as valuable background for the following empirical studies which were the main objective of the dissertation.

The first type of interdependence in the discovery and adoption of Facebook applications was analyzed in **chapter 4.** It presented an individual-level study based on data from an online survey that examined to which extent social influence and the perception of network effects impact the decisions of users of Facebook applications. The two decisions under investigation were (1) the decision to adopt and use an application and (2) the decision of whether to promote and exert influence on friends to also use the application. The results showed that the strongest determinant of the adoption of Facebook applications is whether users perceive that peers are using the application as well. If they are additionally actively influenced by their peers to use the application, the probability of adoption increases further. I also found that the perception of local, but not the one of global, network effects has a positive influence on the adoption decision. With regard to a user's decision to promote an application or not, the findings are consistent with previous research. While the perception of global network effects does not significantly influence an individual to actively recommend an application to peers, the perception of local network effects does have a significant, strong positive effect. This is in line with previous theoretical predictions (Henkel & Block 2008). Users in small, local networks are inclined to pull the remaining non-users of the product into using the service. The findings of this study confirmed the expectation that the consumption of Facebook applications is embedded in a highly social context in which users interact and communicate without friction. This has important implications on how products are discovered and adopted.

The interdependence of applications in the discovery and usage of Facebook applications was studied in **chapter 5**. The study was based on the original data set on Facebook applications and examined to which extent information spillovers between applications within the portfolio of one developer exist. Here, different mechanisms in which these information spillovers may occur were discussed conceptually. Furthermore, the method used by Hendricks & Sorensen (2009) was adapted to the context. The results of the analysis show that there are substantive, positive and persistent spillovers from the launch of the second and the third application on the first application in the portfolio. No significant results were obtained for spillovers on second applications. The setup of the empirical approach and the pattern of the estimation results suggest that the lack of information about available applications is a very important source of these spillovers. The effect is stronger than observed in the study by Hendricks & Sorensen (2009) on albums of recorded music. This is surprising because one would expect that the costs of searching for alternative options decreases in a digital environment. The supply of applications, however, appears to be so overwhelming that users mainly rely in their selection of new applications on their peers (see chapter 4) or some form of communication by the developer of other applications.

Implications and further research questions were discussed in the respective summaries of the chapters. Thus, I conclude this dissertation by discussing the contribution of these findings to the debate about market structure in internet-enabled markets.

Contribution to the debate on market structure in internet-enabled industries

The impact of internet on market structure is the focus of many recent studies (Brynjolfsson et al. 2003; Fleder & Hosanagar 2009; Oestreicher-Singer & Sundararajan 2009). For example, this research is motivated by reduced costs of product search and the increasing proliferation of the digitization of word-of-mouth processes (Dellarocas 2003). With regards to social interaction, there are two opposing lines of argumentation (Dellarocas & Narayan 2007). On the one hand, the opportunity for users to easily discuss and recommend even largely unknown products will shift demand towards the "long tail" of less popular products (Anderson 2006). The underlying hypothesis is that such forms of communication reduce the informational inequality between hit and niche products and help other consumers discover products otherwise consigned to the "long tail", resulting in less concentrated markets. On the other hand, it has been argued that other drivers, such as user-generated rankings and the prevalence of prominently displayed statistics about other consumers' actions (Duan et al. 2006; Tucker & Zhang 2009) will lead to bandwagon behavior, directing consumer attention to already popular products - a phenomenon referred to as the "superstar effect" (Rosen 2011). Indeed, Boudreau & Hagiu (2010) suggest that platform operators like Facebook regulate the market for applications such that winner-takes-all outcomes arise in niches to incentivize developers to contribute high quality applications.

The findings of the study on individual level decisions support the argumentation for an increased likelihood of bandwagon processes. Social influence, both passive and active, are dominant determinants of a user's decision to adopt an application. Since some applications in addition seem to exhibit increasing returns the more friends are using it, positive and reinforcing processes are likely. My study on spillovers between applications suggests that the sizeable lack of information of the available options contributes further, besides other factors such as quality differences, to a highly skewed distribution of success in the market for applications.

Highly concentrated markets oftentimes bring economic welfare loss (Hendricks & Sorensen 2009). The lack of information about obscure applications represents a welfare loss for individuals who would prefer to use less popular applications if they knew about them. It may also disincentivize developers to build applications that appeal only to few users because they will be difficult to find. This could lead to a focus on mass-compatible applications and, thus, a decrease in product variety. While the costs of developing a professional applications or recording a song are roughly the same (The Economist 2010), entry barriers appear to be lower now than they were in the music industry at the time of the study by Hendricks & Sorensen (2009). Furthermore, costs of distribution and marketing are arguably significantly lower. Developers are also not nearly as reliable on one single medium (i.e. the radio in the case of music before the internet) as the channel for discovery. Even though more popular applications are more likely to be discovered by a circle of friends and disseminated within the group, it is now easier to "seed" a new product and support early users to pass it on to friends.

In conclusion, interdependencies in the discovery and adoption of applications on Facebook's platform are facilitating winners to take all – but that does not imply that everyone loses.

References

Abrahamson, E. & Rosenkopf, L., 1997. Social network effects on the extent of innovation diffusion: A computer simulation. *Organization Science*, 8(3), p. 289-309.

Acquisti, A. & Gross, R., 2006. Imagined communities: Awareness, information sharing, and privacy on the Facebook. In G. Danezis & P. Golle, eds. *Privacy Enhancing Technologies*. Berlin, Germany: Springer, p. 36-58.

Ahmed, A., 2011. Goldman-Facebook Deal Raises Debate on Investor Pool. *The New York Times*. Available at: http://dealbook.nytimes.com/2011/01/05/the-500-investor-threshold-debated-for-its-47-year-history/ [Accessed January 19, 2011].

Anderson, C., 2006. *The long tail: Why the Future of Business is Selling Less of More*, New York, NY: Hyperion.

Aral, S. & Walker, D., 2010. Creating Social Contagion through Viral Product Design: A Randomized Trial of Peer Influence in Networks. In *Proceedings of the 31th Annual International Conference on Information Systems*. p. 1-53.

Aral, S., Muchnik, L. & Sundararajan, A., 2009. Distinguishing influence-based contagion from homophily-driven diffusion in dynamic networks. *Proceedings of the National Academy of Sciences of the United States of America*, 106(51), p. 21544-21549.

Arellano, M. & Bond, S., 1991. Some tests of specification for panel data: Monte Carlo evidence and an application to employment equations. *The Review of Economic Studies*, 58(2), p. 277-297.

Armstrong, J.S. & Overton, T.S., 1977. Estimating nonresponse bias in mail surveys. *Journal of Marketing Research*, 14(3), p. 396-402.

Arndt, J., 1967. Role of Product-Related Conversations in the Diffusion of a New Product. *Journal of Marketing Research*, 4(3), p. 291-295.

Arrington, M., 2007. Facebook Launches Facebook Platform - They are the Anti-MySpace. *TechCrunch.com*. Available at: http://techcrunch.com/2007/05/24/facebook-launches-facebook-platform-they-are-the-anti-myspace/ [Accessed September 16, 2010].

Arrington, M., 2009. Zynga Settles Mob Wars Litigation As It Settles In To Playdom Fight. *TechCrunch.com*. Available at: http://techcrunch.com/2009/09/13/zynga-settles-mob-wars-litigation-as-it-settles-in-to-playdom-war/ [Accessed September 6, 2010].

Banerjee, A.V., 1992. A simple model of herd behavior. *The Quarterly Journal of Economics*, 107(3), p. 797-817.

Barash, V. et al., 2010. Faceplant: Impression (Mis) management in Facebook Status Updates. In *Proceedings of the Fourth International AAAI Conference on Weblogs and Social Media*. p. 207-210.

Becker, G.S., 1991. A note on restaurant pricing and other examples of social influences on price. *Journal of Political Economy*, 99(5), p. 1109-1116.

Bernoff, J., 2010. Introducing Peer Influence Analysis: 500 billion peer impressions per year. *Forrester Blog*. Available at: http://forrester.typepad.com/groundswell/2010/04/introducing-peer-influence-analysis.html [Accessed March 12, 2011].

Bikhchandani, S. & Hirschleifer, D., 1992. A theory of fads, fashion, custom, and cultural change as informational cascades. *Journal of Political Economy*, 100(5), p. 992-1026.

Bikhchandani, S., Hirshleifer, D. & Welch, I., 1998. Learning from the Behavior of Others: Conformity, Fads, and Informational Cascades. *The Journal of Economic Perspectives*, 12(3), p. 151-170.

Block, J.H. & Koellinger, P., 2007. Peer Influence in Network Markets: An Empirical Investigation. *Schmalenbach Business Review*, 59(4), p. 364-386.

Boudreau, K.J., 2008a. Opening the platform vs. opening the complementary good? The effect on product innovation in handheld computing. *SSRN Working Paper*, No. 1251167 (available at: http://papers.ssrn.com/abstract_id=1251167), p. 1-36.

Boudreau, K.J., 2008b. Too many complementors? *SSRN Working Paper*, No. 943088 (available at: http://papers.ssrn.com/abstract_id=943088), p. 1-38.

Boudreau, K.J. & Hagiu, A., 2010. Platforms rules: multi-sided platforms as regulators. In A. Gawer, ed. *Platform, Markets and Innovation*. Cheltenham (UK): Edward Elgar Publishing, p. 163-191.

Boudreau, K.J., Lacetera, N. & Lakhani, K.R., 2008. Parallel search, incentives and problem type: Revisiting the competition and innovation link. *Harvard Business School Working Paper*, No. 09-041 (available at: http://www.hbs.edu/research/pdf/09-041.pdf), p. 1-41.

Boyd, D.M. & Ellison, N.B., 2007. Social Network Sites: Definition, History, and Scholarship. *Journal of Computer-Mediated Communication*, 13(1), article 11.

Brynjolfsson, E., Hu, Y.J. & Smith, M.D., 2003. Consumer Surplus in the Digital Economy: Estimating the Value of Increased Product Variety at Online Booksellers. *Management Science*, 49(11), p. 1580-1596.

Brynjolfsson, E., Hu, Y.J. & Smith, M.D., 2006. From niches to riches: Anatomy of the long tail. *MIT Sloan Management Review*, 47(4), p. 67-71.

Bulte, C. Van den & Stremersch, S., 2004. Social Contagion and Income Heterogeneity in New Product Diffusion: A Meta-Analytic Test. *Marketing Science*, 23(4), p. 530-544.

Cabral, L., 2000. Stretching firm and brand reputation. *Rand Journal of Economics*, 31(4), p. 658-673.

Cai, H., Chen, Y. & Fang, H., 2009. Observational Learning: Evidence from a Randomized Natural Field Experiment. *The American Economic Review*, 99(3), p. 864–882.

Cameron, A. & Trivedi, P., 2005. *Microeconometrics*, New York, NY: Cambridge University Press.

Cameron, A. & Trivedi, P., 2009. *Microeconometrics using Stata*, College Station, TX: Stata Press.

Chen, Y. & Xie, J., 2008. Online Consumer Review: Word-of-Mouth as a New Element of Marketing Communication Mix. *Management Science*, 54(3), p. 477-491.

Choi, J.P., 1998. Brand extension as informational leverage. *Review of Economic Studies*, 65(4), p. 655-669.

Church, J. & Gandal, N., 1992. Network effects, software provision, and standardization. *The Journal of Industrial Economics*, 40(1), p. 85-103.

Cieply, M. & Barnes, B., 2011. "The Social Network" Dominates Golden Globes. *The New York Times*. Available at: http://www.nytimes.com/2011/01/17/movies/awardsseason/17globes.html [Accessed January 20, 2011].

Claussen, J., Kretschmer, T. & Mayrhofer, P., 2010. Private Regulation by Platform Operators - Implications for Usage Intensity. *SSRN Working Paper*, No. 1599458 (available at: http://ssrn.com/paper=1599458), p. 1-35.

Corrocher, N. & Zirulia, L., 2009. Me and you and everyone we know: An empirical analysis of local network effects in mobile communications. *Telecommunications Policy*, 33(1), p. 68-79.

Cox, D., 1972. Regression models and life-tables. *Journal of the Royal Statistical Society*, 34(2), p. 187-220.

Craig, S. & Sorkin, A.R., 2011. Goldman Invests in Facebook at $50 Billion Valuation. *The New York Times*. Available at: http://dealbook.nytimes.com/2011/01/02/goldman-invests-in-facebook-at-50-billion-valuation/ [Accessed January 19, 2011].

Crunchbase, 2011. Facebook. *Crunchbase*. Available at: http://www.crunchbase.com/company/facebook [Accessed January 27, 2011].

Dellarocas, C., 2003. The Digitization of Word of Mouth: Promise and Challenges of Online Feedback Mechanisms. *Management Science*, 49(10), p. 1407-1424.

Dellarocas, C. & Narayan, R., 2007. Tall heads vs. long tails: Do consumer reviews increase the informational inequality between hit and niche products. *Robert H. Smith School of Business Research Working Paper*, No. 06-056 (available at: http://ssrn.com/paper=1105956), p. 1-38.

Deutsch, M. & Gerard, H.B., 1955. A study of normative and informational social influences upon individual judgement. *Journal of Abnormal and Social Psychology*, 51(3), p. 629-636.

DiMicco, J.M. & Millen, D.R., 2007. Identity management: multiple presentations of self in facebook. In *Proceedings of the 2007 international ACM conference on Supporting group work*. ACM, p. 383-386.

Duan, W., Gu, B. & Whinston, A.B., 2006. Herd Behavior and Software Adoption on the Internet: An Empirical Investigation. *SSRN Working Paper*, No. 872576 (available at: http://ssrn.com/paper=872576), p. 1-51.

Dwyer, C., Hiltz, S.R. & Passerini, K., 2007. Trust and privacy concern within social networking sites: A comparison of Facebook and MySpace. *Proceedings of AMCIS*, p. 1-12.

D'Aveni, R., 1994. *Hypercompetition*, New York, NY: Free Press.

Eisenmann, T.R. et al., 2009. Facebook's Platforms. *Harvard Business School Case*, No. 9-808-128, p. 1-29.

Eisenmann, T.R. et al., 2006. Strategies for two-sided markets. *Harvard Business Review*, 84(10), p. 92-104.

Eldon, E., 2007. Q&A with iLike's Ali Partovi on Facebook. *VentureBeat*. Available at: http://venturebeat.com/2007/05/29/qa-with-ilikes-ali-partovi-on-facebook/ [Accessed September 6, 2010].

Ellison, G. & Ellison, S.F., 2005. Lessons About Markets from the Internet. *Journal of Economic Perspectives*, 19(2), p. 139-158.

Ermecke, R., Mayrhofer, P. & Wagner, S., 2009. Agents of Diffusion - Insights from a Survey of Facebook Users. In *42nd Hawaii International Conference on System Sciences, 2009*. p. 1-10.

Evans, D.S., 2008. The economics of the online advertising industry. *Review of Network Economics*, 7(3), p. 359-391.

Evans, D.S., Hagiu, A. & Schmalensee, R., 2006. *Invisible Engines: How Software Platforms Drive Innovation and Transform Industries*, Cambridge, MA: The MIT Press.

Facebook, 2007a. A Shift to Engagement. *Facebook Developer Blog*. Available at: https://developers.facebook.com/blog/post/30 [Accessed March 10, 2011].

Facebook, 2007b. Change is Coming. *Facebook Developer Blog*. Available at: https://developers.facebook.com/blog/post/29 [Accessed March 10, 2011].

Facebook, 2008a. Changes to the Application About Page. *Facebook Developer Blog*. Available at: https://developers.facebook.com/blog/post/71 [Accessed March 10, 2011].

Facebook, 2011a. Facebook Company Timeline. *Facebook Press Room - Company Timeline*. Available at: http://www.facebook.com/press/info.php?timeline [Accessed January 30, 2011].

Facebook, 2011b. Facebook Credits. *Facebook.com*. Available at: https://www.facebook.com/credits/ [Accessed March 10, 2011].

Facebook, 2007c. Facebook Platform Launches. *Facebook Developer Blog*. Available at: https://developers.facebook.com/blog/post/21 [Accessed March 10, 2011].

Facebook, 2007d. Facebook Platform Launches with 65 Developer Partners and Over 85 Applications for Facebook. *Facebook.com*. Available at: http://www.facebook.com/press/releases.php?p=1319 [Accessed September 16, 2010].

Facebook, 2008b. Facebook Platform Policy. *Facebook Developer Blog*. Available at: https://developers.facebook.com/blog/post/82 [Accessed March 10, 2011].

Facebook, 2011c. Facebook Statistics. *Facebook Press Room - Statistics*. Available at: http://www.facebook.com/press/info.php?statistics [Accessed January 27, 2011].

Facebook, 2008c. Forced Invites and Unwelcome Communications. *Facebook Developer Blog*. Available at: https://developers.facebook.com/blog/post/86 [Accessed March 10, 2011].

Facebook, 2007e. Mark Zuckerberg Keynote Speech f8 2007. *Facebook Corporate Videos*. Available at: https://www.facebook.com/video/video.php?v=28202665043 [Accessed March 10, 2011].

Facebook, 2007f. Misleading Notifications To Users Will Be Blocked. *Facebook Developer Blog*. Available at: https://developers.facebook.com/blog/post/26 [Accessed March 10, 2011].

Facebook, 2008d. New Year. New Rules. *Facebook Developer Blog*. Available at: https://developers.facebook.com/blog/post/63 [Accessed March 10, 2011].

Facebook, 2007g. News Feed Improvements. *Facebook Developer Blog*. Available at: https://developers.facebook.com/blog/post/55 [Accessed March 10, 2011].

Facebook, 2008e. Simpler, More Relevant Profiles. *Facebook Developer Blog*. Available at: https://developers.facebook.com/blog/post/87 [Accessed March 10, 2011].

Facebook, 2008f. Upcoming Changes to User Profiles. *Facebook Developer Blog*. Available at: https://developers.facebook.com/blog/post/64 [Accessed March 10, 2011].

Farrell, J. & Saloner, G., 1986. Installed base and compatibility: Innovation, product preannouncements, and predation. *The American Economic Review*, 76(5), p. 940-955.

fbFund, 2011. fbFund. *fbFund*. Available at: http://fbfund.com/about/ [Accessed January 29, 2011]

Feick, L.F. & Price, L.L., 1987. The Market Maven: A Diffuser of Marketplace Information. *Journal of Marketing*, 51(1), p. 83-97.

Fleder, D. & Hosanagar, K., 2009. Blockbuster Culture's Next Rise or Fall: The Impact of Recommender Systems on Sales Diversity. *Management Science*, 55(5), p. 697-712.

Freiert, M., 2007. 14 million people interacted with Facebook Applications in August. *Compete Web Page*. Available at: http://blog.compete.com/2007/09/14/facebook-activity-breakdown-application/ [Accessed March 10, 2011].

Gawer, A. & Cusumano, M.A., 2002. *Platform Leadership: How Intel, Microsoft, and Cisco Drive Industry Innovation*, Boston, MA: Harvard Business Press.

Gjoka, M. et al., 2010. Walking in Facebook: A Case Study of Unbiased Sampling of OSNs. In *2010 Proceedings IEEE INFOCOM*. IEEE, p. 1-9.

Gjoka, M. et al., 2008. Poking facebook: characterization of osn applications. In *Proceedings of the first workshop on Online social networks*. ACM, p. 31-36.

Godes, D. & Mayzlin, D., 2009. Firm-Created Word-of-Mouth Communication: Evidence from a Field Test. *Marketing Science*, 28(4), p. 721-739.

Godes, D. & Mayzlin, D., 2004. Using Online Conversations to Study Word-of-Mouth Communication. *Marketing Science*, 23(4), p. 545-560.

Godes, D. et al., 2005. The firm's management of social interactions. *Marketing Letters*, 16(3), p. 415-428.

Golder, P.N. & Tellis, G.J., 1993. Pioneer advantage: Marketing logic or marketing legend? *Journal of Marketing Research*, 30(2), p. 158-170.

Goldman, J., 2008. *Facebook Cookbook: Building Applications to Grow Your Facebook Empire*, Sebastopol, CA: O'Reilly Media.

Granovetter, M., 1973. The strength of weak ties. *The American Journal of Sociology*, 78(6), p. 1360-1380.

Grossman, L., 2010. Mark Zuckerberg - Person of the Year 2010. *TIME Magazine*. Available at: http://www.time.com/time/specials/packages/article/0,28804,2036683_2037183_2037185,00.html [Accessed January 19, 2011].

Günther, O., Krasnova, H. & Koroleva, K., 2010. Stop Spamming Me! - Exploring Information Overload on Facebook. In *AMCIS 2010 Proceedings*. p. 1-10.

Hagiu, A., 2007. Merchant or Two-Sided Platform? *Harvard Business School Working Paper*, No. 07-093 (available at: http://www.hbs.edu/research/pdf/07-093.pdf), p. 1-19.

Harrison-Walker, L.J., 2001. The Measurement of Word-of-Mouth Communication and an Investigation of Service Quality and Customer Commitment As Potential Antecedents. *Journal of Service Research*, 4(1), p. 60-75.

Hendricks, K. & Sorensen, A.T., 2006. Information Spillovers in the Market for Recorded Music. *SSRN Working Paper*, No. 905520 (available at: http://ssrn.com/paper=905520), p. 1-43.

Hendricks, K. & Sorensen, A.T., 2009. Information and the skewness of music sales. *Journal of Political Economy*, 117(2), p. 324-368.

Hendricks, K., Sorensen, A.T. & Wiseman, T., 2009. Observational Learning and Demand for Search Goods. *Stanford University Working Paper*, available at: http://www.stanford.edu/~asorense/papers/hendricks_sorensen_wiseman_2010.pd f, p. 1-39.

Hendrickson, M., 2007. Facebook Apps Are Pointless If They Don't Work. *TechCrunch.com*. Available at: http://techcrunch.com/2007/09/12/facebook-apps-are-pointless-if-they-dont-work/ [Accessed September 6, 2010].

Henkel, J. & Block, J.H., 2008. Peer Influence in Network Markets: An Empirical and Theoretical Analysis. *SSRN Working Paper*, No. 956564 (available at: http://ssrn.com/paper=956564), p. 1-28.

Hervas-Drane, A., 2009. Word of Mouth and Taste Matching : A Theory of the Long Tail. *NET Institute Working Paper*, No. 07-41 (available at: http://ideas.repec.org/p/net/wpaper/0741.html), p. 1-36.

Hill, S., Provost, F. & Volinsky, C., 2006. Network-Based Marketing: Identifying Likely Adopters via Consumer Networks. *Statistical Science*, 21(2), p. 256-276.

Hippel, E. Von, 1988. *The sources of innovation*, New York, NY: Oxford University Press.

Inside Facebook, 2011. About Inside Facebook. *insidefacebook.com*. Available at: http://www.insidefacebook.com/about/ [Accessed January 29, 2011].

Joinson, A.N., 2008. Looking at, looking up or keeping up with people?: motives and use of Facebook. In *Proceeding of the twenty-sixth annual SIGCHI conference on Human factors in computing systems*. ACM, p. 1027-1036.

Joyent, 2011. Free Facebook Developer Program. *Joyent Homepage*. Available at: http://www.joyentcloud.com/developers/free-facebook-developer-program/ [Accessed January 29, 2011].

Katz, E. & Lazarsfeld, P.F., 1955. *Personal influence: The part played by people in the flow of mass communications*, New York, NY: Free Press.

Katz, M.L. & Shapiro, C., 1985. Network externalities, competition, and compatibility. *The American Economic Review*, 75(3), p. 424-440.

Katz, M.L. & Shapiro, C., 1994. Systems competition and network effects. *The Journal of Economic Perspectives*, 8(2), p. 93-115.

Katz, M.L. & Shapiro, C., 1986. Technology Adoption in the Presence of Network Externalities. *Journal of Political Economy*, 94(4), p. 822-841.

Keller, J., 2009. *Empirical analysis of developers of complementary applications to an online programming platform*. Fakultät für Wirtschaftswissenschaften, Technische Universität München, unpublished diploma thesis.

Kirkpatrick, D., 2010. *Facebook Effect: The Inside Story Of The Company That Is Connecting The World*, New York, NY: Simon & Schuster.

Koski, H. & Kretschmer, T., 2004. Survey on Competing in Network Industries: Firm Strategies, Market Outcomes, and Policy Implications. *Journal of Industry, Competition and Trade*, 4(1), p. 5-31.

Kretschmer, M., Klimis, G.M. & Choi, C.J., 1999. Increasing Returns and Social Contagion in Cultural Industries. *British Journal of Management*, 10, p. 61-72.

Lampe, C., Ellison, N.B. & Steinfield, C., 2006. A Face (book) in the Crowd : Social Searching vs . Social Browsing. *Human Factors*, p. 167-170.

Lampe, C., Ellison, N.B. & Steinfield, C., 2007. A familiar face (book): profile elements as signals in an online social network. In *Proceedings of the SIGCHI conference on Human factors in computing systems*. ACM, p. 435-444.

Lee, E., 2007. Widgets add flair to dress up Web sites / MySpace, Facebook members among first to adopt method of adding personal touches - SFGate. *SF Gate*. Available at: http://articles.sfgate.com/2007-09-03/business/17263249_1_ilike-palo-alto-s-facebook-widgets [Accessed February 2, 2011].

Li, Y.-M. & Hsiao, H.-W., 2009. Recommender Service for Social Network based Applications. *International Conference on Electronic Commerce*, p. 378-381.

Lohr, S., 2009. For Today's Graduate, Just One Word - Statistics. *The New York Times*. Available at: http://www.nytimes.com/2009/08/06/technology/06stats.html [Accessed December 31, 2010].

López, L.E. & Roberts, E.B., 2002. First-mover advantages in regimes of weak appropriability: the case of financial services innovations. *Journal of Business Research*, 55(12), p. 997-1005.

Makadok, R., 1998. Can first-mover and early-mover advantages be sustained in an industry with low barriers to entry/imitation? *Strategic Management Journal*, 19(7), p. 683-696.

Mason, W.A., Conrey, F.R. & Smith, E.R., 2007. Situating social influence processes: Dynamic, multidirectional flows of influence within social networks. *Personality and Social Psychology Review*, 11(3), p. 279-300.

Mayrhofer, P. & Keller, J., 2011. Guide to the "Facebook Platform", unpublished white paper, available upon request from mayrhofer@cdtm.de.

Mayzlin, D., 2006. Promotional chat on the Internet. *Marketing Science*, 25(2), p. 155-163.

Moretti, E., 2009. Social learning and peer effects in consumption: Evidence from movie sales. *NBER Working Paper*, No. W13832 (available at: http://ssrn.com/paper=1104169), p. 1-46.

Naaman, M., Boase, J. & Lai, C.-H., 2010. Is it really about me?: message content in social awareness streams. In *Proceedings of CSCW 2010*. ACM.

Nault, B.R. & Vandenbosch, M.B., 1996. Eating your own lunch: Protection through preemption. *Organization Science*, 7(3), p. 342-358.

Nazir, A., Raza, S. & Chuah, C., 2008. Unveiling facebook: a measurement study of social network based applications. In *Proceedings of the 8th ACM SIGCOMM conference on Internet measurement*. ACM, p. 43–56.

Oestreicher-Singer, G. & Sundararajan, A., 2009. Recommendation networks and the long tail of electronic commerce. *NET Institute Working Papers*, No. 09-03 (available at: http://ideas.repec.org/p/net/wpaper/0903.html), p. 1-35.

Oestreicher-Singer, G. & Sundararajan, A., 2008. The visible hand of social networks in electronic markets. *SSRN Working Paper*, No. 1268516 (available at: http://ssrn.com/paper= 1268516), p. 1-48.

Onnela, J.-P. & Reed-Tsochas, F., 2010. Spontaneous emergence of social influence in online systems. *Proceedings of the National Academy of Sciences*, 107(43), p. 18375-18380.

Oxford Dictionaries Online, 2011. Definition of "interdependent." *Oxford Dictionaries Online*. Available at: http://oxforddictionaries.com/view/entry/m_en_us1258555#m_en_us1258555.006 [Accessed February 2, 2011].

Parker, G.G. & Alstyne, M.W. Van, 2005. Two-Sided Network Effects: A Theory of Information Product Design. *Management Science*, 51(10), p. 1494-1504.

Patel, S., 2007. Making Facebook Platform Apps Scale on the Cheap. *GigaOM.com*. Available at: http://gigaom.com/2007/09/11/making-facebook-platform-apps-scale-on-the-cheap/ [Accessed September 6, 2010].

Rochet, J.-C. & Tirole, J., 2006. Two-Sided Markets: A Progress Report. *The RAND Journal of Economics*, 37(3), p. 645667.

Rogers, E.M., 1983. *Diffusion of innovations*, New York, NY: Free Press.

Rohlfs, J., 1974. A Theory of Interdependent Demand for a Communications Service. *The Bell Journal of Economics and Management Science*, 5(1), p. 16-37.

Rosen, S., 2011. The Economics of Superstars. *American Economic Review*, 71(5), p. 845-858.

Roztocki, N., 2001. Using internet-based surveys for academic research: opportunities and problems. In *Proceedings of the 2001 American Society of Engneering Management (ASEM) National Conference*. ASEM, p. 290-295.

Rusli, E., 2010. Zynga CTO On Moving Mountains Of Data (TCTV). *TechCrunch.com*. Available at: http://techcrunch.com/2010/09/22/zynga-cto-on-moving-mountains-of-data-tctv/ [Accessed September 23, 2010].

Saint, N., 2010. Zynga's Secret To Success: Steal Great Ideas! *The Business Insider*. Available at: http://www.businessinsider.com/how-zynga-is-just-like-microsoft-2010-1 [Accessed August 27, 2010].

Schonfeld, E., 2008. Hints of a Facebook Operating System In New Design. *TechCrunch.com*. Available at: http://techcrunch.com/2008/05/23/hints-of-a-facebook-operating-system-in-new-design/ [Accessed March 10, 2011].

Shapiro, C. & Varian, H.R., 1999. *Information rules: a strategic guide to the network economy*, Boston, MA: Harvard Business Press.

Sheth, J., Mittal, B. & Newman, B.I., 1999. *Customer behavior: consumer behavior and beyond*, Fort Worth, TX: Dryden Press.

Stephen, A.T. & Berger, J.A., 2009. Creating Contagious: How Social Networks and Item Characteristics Combine to Drive Persistent Social Epidemics. *SSRN Working Paper*, No. 1354803 (available at: http://ssrn.com/paper=1354803), p. 1-48.

Stutzman, F., 2010. Implicit Factors in Networked Information Feeds. In *HCIR 2010*. p. 1-4.

Subramani, M. & Rajagopalan, B., 2003. Knowledge-sharing and influence in online social networks via viral marketing. *Communications of the ACM*, 46(12), p. 300-307.

Sun, E. et al., 2009. Gesundheit! - Modeling contagion through Facebook News Feed. In *Proceedings of International AAAI on Weblogs and Social Media*. p. 1-8.

Tansley, S., 2009. *The Fourth Paradigm: Data-Intensive Scientific Discovery*, Microsoft Research.

The Economist, 2007. Face value: Book value. *The Economist*. Available at: http://www.economist.com/node/9507260 [Accessed January 27, 2011].

The Economist, 2010. Growth in mobile applications: Apps and downs. *The Economist*. Available at: http://www.economist.com/node/16381330?story_id=16381330 [Accessed July 19, 2010].

Tirole, J., 1988. *The Theory of Industrial Organization*, Cambridge, MA: MIT Press.

Trusov, M., Bucklin, R.E. & Pauwels, K., 2009. Effects of Word-of-Mouth Versus Traditional Marketing: Findings from an Internet Social Networking Site. *Journal of Marketing*, 73(5), p. 90-102.

Tucker, C. & Zhang, J., 2010. Growing two-sided networks by advertising the user base: A field experiment. *Marketing Science*, 29(5), p. 805-814.

Tucker, C. & Zhang, J., 2009. How does popularity information affect choices? A field experiment. *MIT Sloan School of Management Working Paper*, p. 1-36.

Valente, T.W., 1996. Network models of the diffusion of innovations. *Computational and Mathematical Organization Theory*, 2(2), p. 163-164.

VanderWerf, P.A. & Mahon, J.F., 1997. Meta-analysis of the impact of research methods on findings of first-mover advantage. *Management Science*, 43(11), p. 1510-1519.

Wagner, R., 2008. *Building Facebook Applications For Dummies*, Hoboken, NJ: Wiley Publishing.

Walther, J.B. et al., 2008. The Role of Friends' Appearance and Behavior on Evaluations of Individuals on Facebook: Are We Known by the Company We Keep? *Human Communication Research*, 34(1), p. 28-49.

Wernerfelt, B., 1988. Umbrella Branding as a Signal of New Product Quality: An Example of Signalling by Posting a Bond. *The RAND Journal of Economics*, 19(3), p. 458-466.

Wiedmann, K.P., Walsh, G. & Mitchell, V.W., 2001. The Mannmaven: an agent for diffusing market information. *Journal of Marketing Communications*, 7(4), p. 195-212.

Wooldridge, J., 2002. *Econometric analysis of cross section and panel data*, Cambridge, MA: MIT Press.

Zhao, S., Grasmuck, S. & Martin, J., 2008. Identity construction on Facebook: Digital empowerment in anchored relationships. *Computers in Human Behavior*, 24(5), p. 1816-1836.

Appendix

A.   Appendix for chapter 3

Table 22: Summary statistics of application usage (by time on platform)

At week	N	Mean	SD	P5	P25	Median	P75	P95	Min	Max
Installations per application at week										
2	2663	20313	156030	115	423	1048	4201	60350	6	5645121
4	2648	45854	232974	298	1017	2668	12143	178808	9	6745367
8	2543	79982	331887	606	1813	4986	21600	359400	25	6422660
12	2370	114914	707842	789	2300	6462	27807	409020	75	20915474
16	1976	124103	564717	845	2557	6896	29217	511171	100	12987166
20	1450	136151	544403	880	2600	7036	31950	640439	100	6163167
Daily active users per application at week										
2	2667	3113	15369	19	82	201	776	11534	0	307482
4	2667	3826	16546	16	66	190	955	15977	0	260082
8	2668	3829	20200	8	52	163	700	12838	0	375255
12	2667	3636	22676	5	39	124	573	10368	0	528185
16	2467	3550	25540	4	26	99	460	8941	0	672454
20	2003	3783	30084	2	19	86	385	7988	0	739580
Percent active users per application at										
2	2667	22.81	12.97	4.75	13.00	21.14	30.71	46.83	0	94.00
4	2667	9.31	7.14	1.57	4.17	7.60	12.33	23.43	0	57.80
8	2668	4.68	5.05	0.17	1.50	3.00	5.83	14.75	0	42.17
12	2667	3.02	3.97	0.00	1.00	1.83	3.67	10.57	0	40.86
16	2467	2.25	3.32	0.00	0.50	1.00	2.67	8.33	0	38.25
20	2003	1.81	2.97	0.00	0.00	1.00	2.00	7.43	0	33.25

Table 23: Summary statistics of developer success (by time on platform)

At week	N	Mean	SD	P5	P25	Median	P75	P95	Min	Max
Installations per developer at week										
2	2060	28543	228808	75	392	926	3403	56812	0	6156516
4	2142	54733	415401	153	880	2239	8700	143918	0	8851400
8	2263	74651	376078	0	1318	4029	16000	310400	0	9650524
12	2371	107777	554106	0	1323	4700	21124	474854	0	12810240
16	2228	119477	587441	0	1088	4200	23038	502925	0	14933310
20	1907	134172	596570	0	844	4277	24100	588700	0	6684922
Daily active users per developer at week										
2	2060	2742	17224	16	72	159	533	7930	0	307482
4	2142	3740	20504	13	60	166	690	13082	0	348932
8	2263	4405	22365	6	49	154	713	17711	0	336477
12	2371	5044	28898	5	38	124	683	15863	0	389933
16	2228	5318	31412	4	29	111	632	16495	0	598517
20	1907	5983	35669	3	25	113	652	17038	0	661303
Percent active users per developer at										
2	2060	21.77	15.11	2.00	10.07	19.41	31.00	48.63	0.00	100.00
4	2142	10.25	9.39	1.00	3.83	7.71	13.71	27.00	0.00	83.00
8	2263	6.15	8.03	0.00	1.60	3.50	7.21	21.00	0.00	76.00
12	2371	4.29	6.98	0.00	1.00	2.00	4.83	16.00	0.00	86.00
16	2228	3.56	6.75	0.00	0.75	1.50	3.67	14.33	0.00	100.00
20	1907	3.05	5.42	0.00	0.50	1.17	3.14	12.57	0.00	60.60

Table 24: Summary statistics portfolio vs. single-app developers.

Variable	PD	N	Mean	SD	Diff[a,b]	P5	P25	Median	P75	P95	Min	Max
company (0/1)	0	2207	0.38		***						0	1
	1	452	0.25								0	1
entry week	0	2207	2007w47	10	***	2007w27	2007w41	2007w47	2008w4	2008w11	2007w27	2008w15
	1	452	2007w42	9		2007w27	2007w35	2007w42	2007w48	2008w6	2007w27	2008w12
entry before Sep 07 (0/1)	0	2207	0.11		***						0	1
	1	452	0.23								0	1
installations before Sep 07 (in 000s)	0	2207	34.272	673.307	***	0.000	0.000	0.000	0.000	0.823	0.000	22248.230
	1	452	122.095	627.377		0.000	0.000	0.000	0.000	355.833	0.000	6487.595
number of apps (before Sep 07)	0	2207	0.15	1.23	***	0.00	0.00	0.00	0.00	1.00	0.00	50.00
	1	452	0.60	1.91		0.00	0.00	0.00	0.00	4.00	0.00	23.00
maximum daily active usage of all apps by developer (in 000s)	0	2207	7184	39967	***	104	163	384	1408	21823	1	661303
	1	452	29279	77004		263	915	3676	20339	130255	125	824494
total accum. daily active usage of all apps per dev (in 000)	0	2207	96.202	645.069	***	0.451	1.282	3.265	11.892	249.957	0.135	11908.671
	1	452	346.544	1002.826		2.417	10.928	41.698	238.970	1471.086	0.502	11616.982

Note: PD denotes whether a developer is a portfolio developer or not. The test on inequality is based on [a]independent samples t-tests and [b]Chi-square tests. *** denotes significance at the 1% level.

Table 25: Correlation matrix for variables of elapsed time analysis

Variable	(1)	(2)	(3)	(4)	(5)	(6)	(7)	(8)	(9)	(10)	(11)	(12)	(13)	(14)	(15)
(1) first 4 weeks accum. usage (in 100k)	1														
(2) growth rate (in percent)	0.02	1													
(3) number of updates in previous 2 weeks	0.03	0.19	1												
(4) number of updates in previous weeks 2 to 4	-0.04	-0.09	-0.43	1											
(5) company developer (0/1)	0	-0.02	0.1	-0.05	1										
(6) experience at application launch (in weeks)	0.06	-0.05	-0.12	-0.05	0.04	1									
(7) entry before Sept 02, 2007 (0/1)	0.1	-0.04	0.05	0.02	0.12	0.66	1								
(8) num. installs in week 34, 2007 (in million)	0.22	-0.03	-0.02	-0.03	-0.01	0.17	0.23	1							
(9) num. applications in week 34, 2007	0.07	-0.03	0.01	0.04	0.1	0.41	0.62	0.23	1						
(10) application in same category as previous	0.06	-0.03	0.08	0.03	0.01	0.13	0.05	0.02	0.03	1					
(11) entry order	0.09	-0.02	0.13	0.08	0.13	0.51	0.24	0.01	0.19	0.25	1				
(12) entry order (full sample)	-0.01	-0.01	0.16	-0.03	0.13	0.3	0.25	0.05	0.26	0.1	0.57	1			
(13) number of applications in launch week (in '00s)	-0.03	0	-0.14	-0.12	-0.05	0.35	-0.23	-0.1	-0.18	0.11	0.33	0.07	1		
(14) HHI in app launch week	-0.02	0.01	0.17	0.1	0.04	-0.17	0.26	0.09	0.23	-0.12	-0.25	-0.04	-0.73	1	
(15) HHI in application launch week	-0.04	0.01	-0.13	-0.1	-0.04	0.37	-0.2	-0.09	-0.15	0.1	0.33	0.08	0.98	-0.63	1

Note: N=906 apps. Previous application characteristics: (1)-(4); Developer characteristics: (5)-(9); Application characteristics: (10)-(12); Market characteristics: (13)-(15).

B.   Appendix for chapter 4

Table 26: Adoption model: summary statistics for regressors

	Mean	S.D.	Min	Max
Passive: awareness of friends' use (0/1)	0.89		0.00	1.00
Active: invitation received (0/1)	0.70		0.00	1.00
Benefit from local network effects (0/1)	0.39		0.00	1.00
Benefit from global network effects (0/1)	0.25		0.00	1.00
Passive: installations (in Millions)	8.83	5.54	0.08	23.70
Early adopter	2.63	1.32	1.00	5.00
Ease of use	4.13	0.84	1.00	5.00
Privacy concern	2.60	1.43	1.00	5.00
Cost of profile overload	3.32	1.47	1.00	5.00
Cost of time	2.46	1.29	1.00	5.00
Male (0/1)	0.44		0.00	1.00
Respondent age	22.82	4.12	14.00	46.00
Squared: respondent age	537.83	213.62	196.00	2116.00
USA (0/1)	0.32		0.00	1.00
Germany (0/1)	0.34		0.00	1.00

Note: N = 356.

Table 27: Active influence model: summary statistics for regressors

	Mean	S.D.	Min	Max
Benefit from local network effects (0/1)	0.46	0.50	0.00	1.00
Benefit from global network effects (0/1)	0.27	0.45	0.00	1.00
Active: invitation received (0/1)	0.80	0.40	0.00	1.00
Opinion leadership	2.88	0.91	1.00	5.00
Familiarity high (0/1)	0.36	0.48	0.00	1.00
Male (0/1)	0.36	0.48	0.00	1.00
Respondent age	22.77	4.14	14.00	40.00
Squared: respondent age	535.69	202.77	196.00	1600.00
USA (0/1)	0.31	0.46	0.00	1.00
Germany (0/1)	0.35	0.48	0.00	1.00

Note: N = 168.

Table 28: Correlation matrix for variables of adoption model

Variable	(1)	(2)	(3)	(4)	(5)	(6)	(7)	(8)	(9)	(10)	(11)	(12)	(13)	(14)	(15)
(1) Passive: awareness of friends' use (0/1)	1.00														
(2) Active: invitation received (0/1)	0.23	1.00													
(3) Benefit from local network effects (0/1)	-0.10	0.01	1.00												
(4) Benefit from global network effects (0/1)	-0.08	-0.08	0.54	1.00											
(5) Passive: installations (in Millions)	0.11	0.24	0.07	-0.01	1.00										
(6) Early adopter	-0.08	-0.07	0.01	0.12	-0.01	1.00									
(7) Ease of use	0.08	0.09	0.08	-0.07	-0.00	-0.01	1.00								
(8) Privacy concern	-0.21	-0.15	0.02	0.01	-0.06	0.09	-0.09	1.00							
(9) Cost of profile overload	-0.11	-0.11	0.01	-0.06	0.01	0.05	0.04	0.39	1.00						
(10) Cost of time	-0.14	-0.07	0.04	0.02	-0.01	0.11	-0.08	0.33	0.31	1.00					
(11) Male (0/1)	-0.18	-0.07	-0.02	0.00	0.08	0.32	-0.04	0.09	0.07	0.14	1.00				
(12) Respondent age	-0.14	-0.05	-0.04	-0.00	0.01	0.21	-0.07	0.07	-0.10	0.06	0.28	1.00			
(13) Squared: respondent age	-0.13	-0.05	-0.02	0.00	0.01	0.20	-0.06	0.06	-0.10	0.04	0.27	0.99	1.00		
(14) USA (0/1)	0.11	-0.01	0.07	-0.08	-0.02	-0.24	0.21	-0.03	0.18	-0.06	-0.29	-0.21	-0.18	1.00	
(15) Germany (0/1)	-0.10	-0.03	-0.06	-0.00	0.02	0.26	-0.14	0.02	-0.11	0.02	0.27	0.18	0.16	-0.49	1.00

Note: N=365.

C.   Appendix for chapter 5

Table 29: Application categories for sample for information spillover analysis

Category	Frequency	Percent	Cum.
Just for Fun	308	28.33	28.33
Missing	211	19.41	47.75
Gaming	125	11.50	59.25
Dating	73	6.72	65.96
Messaging	59	5.43	71.39
Utility	42	3.86	75.25
Education	34	3.13	78.38
Sports	32	2.94	81.32
Alerts	27	2.48	83.81
Photo	25	2.30	86.11
Fashion	25	2.30	88.41
Chat	24	2.21	90.62
Food and Drink	20	1.84	92.46
Travel	15	1.38	93.84
Music	14	1.29	95.12
Events	12	1.10	96.23
Video	10	0.92	97.15
Politics	9	0.83	97.98
Business	9	0.83	98.80
Money	6	0.55	99.36
File Sharing	5	0.46	99.82
Mobile	2	0.18	100.00
Total	**1,087**	**100.00**	

Table 30: Results of a reduced Cox Model (coefficients)

VARIABLES	(1) elapsed time between 1 and 2	(2) elapsed time between 2 and 3	(3) elapsed time between 3 and 4	(4) elapsed time overall
first 4 weeks accum. usage of prev. app (in 100k)	0.0269	-0.386	0.0658	-0.0478*
	(0.0439)	(0.244)	(0.124)	(0.0254)
growth rate prev. app (in percent)	0.000131***	0.000597***	0.00159***	0.000154***
	(2.47e-05)	(8.31e-05)	(0.000268)	(2.01e-05)
weeks since platform launch	-0.0657***	-0.0712***	-0.0519***	-0.0612***
	(0.00747)	(0.0111)	(0.0143)	(0.00484)
Observations	452	183	99	906
Chi2	458.4	221.3	164.3	528.4
Log likelihood	-2313	-775.1	-367.2	-5295

Note: Robust standard errors in parentheses; *** $p<0.01$, ** $p<0.05$, * $p<0.1$; category dummies included but not displayed. (4) includes but does not display entry order dummies.

Table 31: Results of a reduced Cox Model (marginal effects)

VARIABLES	(1) elapsed time between 1 and 2	(2) elapsed time between 2 and 3	(3) elapsed time between 3 and 4	(4) elapsed time overall
first 4 weeks accum. usage of prev. app (in 100k)	1.027	0.680	1.068	0.953*
	(0.0451)	(0.166)	(0.133)	(0.0242)
growth rate prev. app (in percent)	1.000***	1.001***	1.002***	1.000***
	(2.47e-05)	(8.32e-05)	(0.000268)	(2.01e-05)
weeks since platform launch	0.936***	0.931***	0.949***	0.941***
	(0.00699)	(0.0103)	(0.0135)	(0.00455)
Observations	452	183	99	906
Chi2	458.4	221.3	164.3	528.4
Log likelihood	-2313	-775.1	-367.2	-5295

Note: Robust standard errors in parentheses; *** $p<0.01$, ** $p<0.05$, * $p<0.1$; category dummies included but not displayed. (4) includes but does not display entry order dummies.

Table 32: Fixed-effects panel regression results for backward spillovers

	Fixed-effects panel regression of backwards spillovers		
	(1)	**(2)**	**(3)**
	spillover from 1	*spillover from*	*spillover from*
	application 2 on	*application 3 on 1*	*application 3 on 2*
VARIABLES	(log of daily users)	(log of daily users)	(log of daily users)
indicatorM3	0.309**	0.220	0.176
	(0.131)	(0.167)	(0.247)
indicatorM2	0.337**	0.228	-0.0552
	(0.157)	(0.208)	(0.339)
indicatorM1	0.351*	0.384	0.0152
	(0.195)	(0.234)	(0.397)
indicator0	0.397*	0.597**	0.0760
	(0.225)	(0.262)	(0.462)
indicator1	0.712***	0.750**	0.328
	(0.256)	(0.296)	(0.533)
indicator2	0.751**	0.769**	0.347
	(0.292)	(0.325)	(0.603)
indicator3	0.795**	0.777**	0.386
	(0.322)	(0.355)	(0.679)
indicator4	0.775**	0.772**	0.342
	(0.357)	(0.387)	(0.754)
indicator5	0.811**	0.732*	0.327
	(0.390)	(0.416)	(0.831)
indicator6	0.818*	0.685	0.292
	(0.423)	(0.444)	(0.906)
indicator7	0.825*	0.631	0.280
	(0.458)	(0.477)	(0.986)
indicator8	0.836*	0.664	0.258
	(0.489)	(0.512)	(1.072)
Constant	5.963***	5.864***	7.437***
	(0.546)	(0.675)	(0.856)
Observations	5,718	2,689	2,144
Number of dev-app-pairs	452	182	183
R-squared	0.074	0.095	0.151

Note: Robust standard errors in parentheses; *** $p<0.01$, ** $p<0.05$, * $p<0.1$; time dummies included but not displayed.

Figure 19: Time patterns of backward spillovers (OLS estimation)

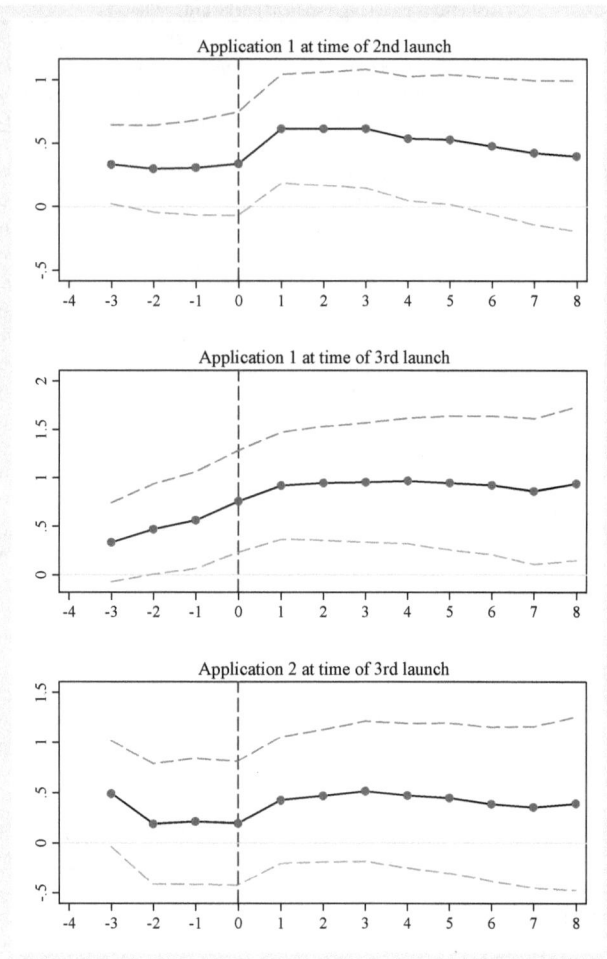

Figure 20: Time patterns of backward spillovers (OLS with additional covariates)

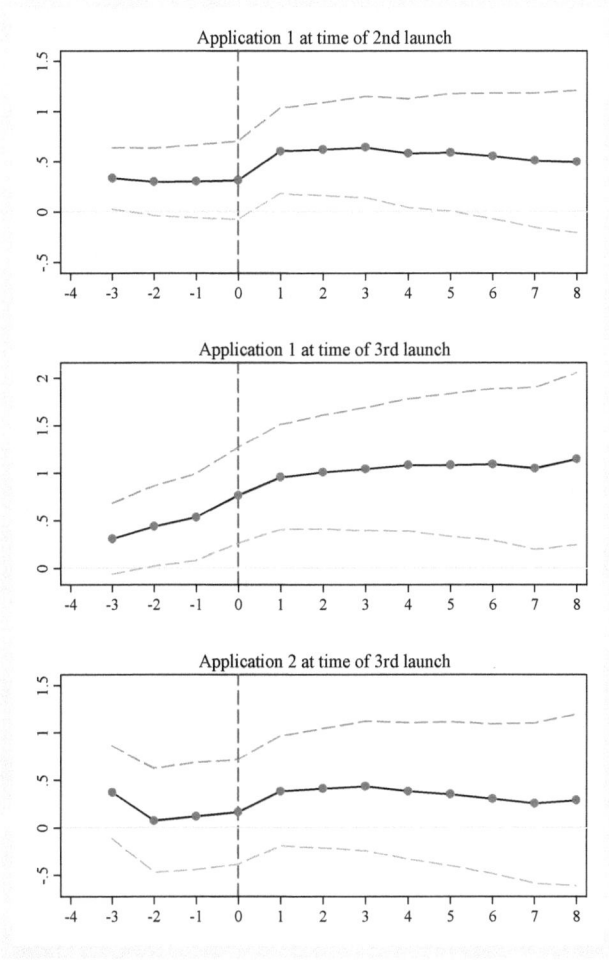

Figure 21: Time patterns of backward spillovers (first-difference panel model)[159]

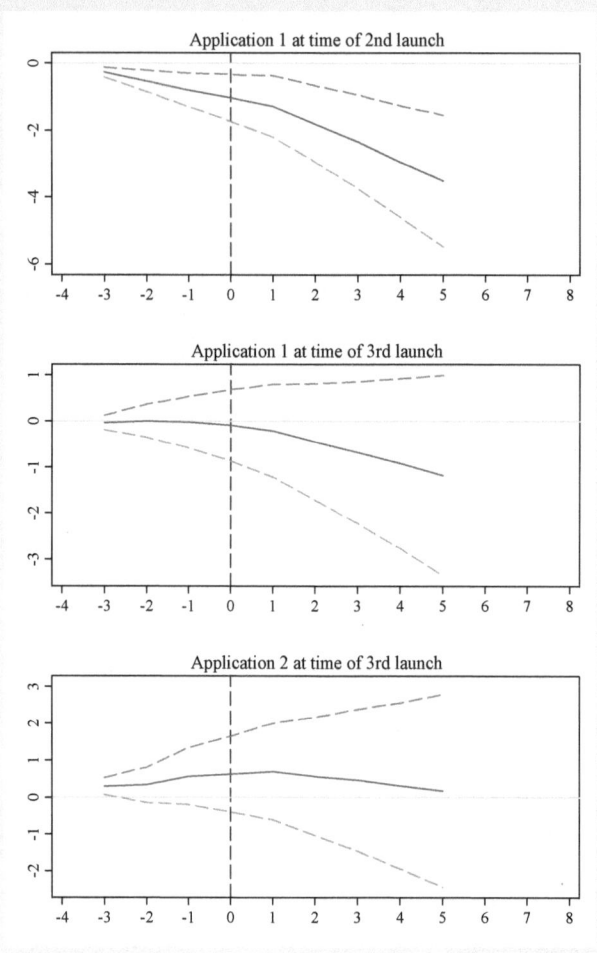